# MAGIC
## FOR BEGINNERS

**How to Order:**

Quantity discounts are available from the publisher, Prima Publishing, P.O. Box 1260MAG, Rocklin, CA 95677; telephone (916) 786-0449. On your letterhead include information concerning the intended use of the books and the number of books you wish to purchase.

*U.S. Bookstores and Libraries:* Please submit all orders to St. Martin's Press, 175 Fifth Avenue, New York, NY 10010; telephone (212) 674-5151.

# MAGIC
## FOR BEGINNERS

**HARRY BARON**

**Illustrated by Dennis Patten**

Prima Publishing
P.O. Box 1260MAG
Rocklin, CA 95677
(916)786-0449

Prima Publishing
Rocklin, CA

Library of Congress Cataloging-in-Publication Data

Baron, Harry. 1919-
  Magic for beginners / by Harry Baron.
    p. cm.
  Reprint. Originally published; New York : Funk &
    Wagnalls, 1968.
  Includes bibliographical references.
  ISBN 1-55958-089-5
  1. Conjuring.  1. Title.
GV1547.B27  1991
793.8—dc20                                    90-48770
                                                   CIP

# CONTENTS

*Introduction*

## 1 MAGIC WITH CARDS

## 2 CLOSE-UP MAGIC

# INTRODUCTION

I have frequently been asked, 'Could I take up magic as a hobby?' - and, whatever the age of the person, I have replied: 'Yes, provided that you are really keen and interested in it.' But of course, it is not just as simple as all that. Where does one learn to do the tricks? How does one go about obtaining magical apparatus? Well, I hope this book will supply the answer.

I have endeavoured to provide the reader with as much knowledge about the subject as is possible within the compass of these pages. Many people are deterred from indulging in this delightful hobby because they think that it is essential to start young, but while it is obviously a good thing to begin in early life, it is not absolutely necessary. In fact there are some leading magicians today who have become eminently successful, yet who only a few years ago had known nothing whatever about magic.

I have attempted to explain *exactly* how to do the tricks in this book, rather than merely to describe them; in fact I have tried to make it just the type of book I would have loved to have acquired myself when I first began in magic.

That magic can be easy to do, is the underlying theme of this book, for in it will be found magic tricks requiring very little apparatus, and all of them calling for no special skill or sleight of hand. Magic can be said to be one of the most rewarding of all hobbies; it can be profitable in many ways.

Firstly, a person who is able to perform conjuring tricks in an entertaining manner, will always be in demand at social functions; also the study of magic principles can be of great use in every day life.

It is international, and the youngest child or even the most primitive savage can appreciate magic in various forms even though no word need be spoken.

It appeals to all ages, and unlike other forms of relaxation the enthusiasm seldom wanes in later life; there are always new tricks to learn and different people to try them on! It is a mental stimulant, encourages acting ability, and fosters inventiveness and adaptability. It teaches you elocution and helps to overcome inferiority complexes, because the very nature of the art requires that it should be presented before other people. Yet the study of conjuring can be pursued when alone, it can be practised in almost any place, and only a second person is needed to form an audience.

Little wonder then that conjuring has such a large following. In England alone there are over eighty magical societies, all with an enthusiastic membership.

The Magic Circle, enjoying a huge membership, was, when it had its centre, equipped with a magnificent library and club rooms. Other great organizations such as the British Ring of the International Brotherhood of Magicians all contribute to the fulfilment of the magical enthusiast.

Magic then is a worthwhile hobby and being so, it deserves newcomers who will be willing to practise the tricks they have acquired, for only assiduous practice will make the student perfect in his presentation.

A maxim which is preached in all text books on magic is, 'never do the same trick twice before the same audience'. There is a very simple reason for this, conjuring effects are not brought about by real magic, there is an explicable *method* behind them. If an audience has already witnessed a trick, it will know what to expect if it is repeated, and knowing this, it will also tend to know when and where to look for the secret. Indeed, many tricks are based on the element of surprise, and if this were absent the effect would lose its value. It will be readily appreciated that a magic trick is no longer a trick if the audience knows how it is done. So, the golden rule is NEVER EXPOSE A TRICK and, tempting though it may sometimes be, never reveal the secret to anyone.

Many years ago, Charles Bertram gave a conjuring show to His Majesty King Edward VII and the Royal Family; King Edward afterwards congratulated Bertram and mentioned that a certain trick had intrigued him - and how was it done?

Bertram resisted the temptation to tell even a king the secret of his trick. Later however, Bertram and King Edward became firm friends and His Majesty developed a great interest in magic, and eventually under Bertram's tuition became quite proficient in the art.

But even though kings themselves lay down the sceptre for the magic wand, the art of magic attracts people from all walks of life. It is not only the lure of the footlights and the applause of an audience but that subtle feeling of well-being and satisfaction in performing a trick which others find a mystery; of being able to achieve something which others cannot. Every reader of this book will have his own idea of what magic will ultimately mean to him. It may lead to entertaining on television or in the village hall, to showing close up tricks to friends or presenting illusions on the stage.

Magic has a long history behind it, and it has progressed through the abracadabra of the Charlatans of the Middle Ages, and on to the hanky-panky of the travelling Mountebank, up to the beginning of the 18th century, when magic as an entertainment really came into its own. That was the heyday of mystery and such names as Herrmann, Houdin, Anderson, Frikell and Heller were names to conjure with. These were the old-time conjurors, when the knowledge of magic was confined to just a few. But the spectacular, full evening displays of magic are fast disappearing, and names like Goldin, Chung-Ling-Soo, Houdini, Kellar, Bertram, Maskelyne and Devant have few counterparts today.

This is the age of TV and cabaret; of fast-moving technique and slick presentations; trap doors, cumbersome tables and heavy drapes are now dispensed with.

Nevertheless there is this great tradition behind it all, and the very name, *Magic*, conjures up an air of mystery in the minds of spectators. So do try to cultivate this aura

3

of illusion by giving your personal enthusiasm; thus you will be able to contribute in a small way to the sum total of human enjoyment.

Near the end of the book will be found a chapter on Misdirection and Presentation. This is one of the most important aspects of magic. It is not enough to know how the tricks are done, you must know how to *present* them properly. There is a world of difference between the two and it is strongly urged that this chapter be given especial study.

The tricks you will read about are those which are used by amateurs and professionals the world over, so I am sure that the absolute beginner and the most advanced performer alike will find a wealth of 'usable material' among these pages.

---

# CHAPTER 1 - MAGIC WITH CARDS

Of all the many aspects of conjuring, the subject of card magic is one of the most popular. Card tricks appeal to most people, and from the performer's point of view, the apparatus required is very simple. Usually a pack of cards is all that is necessary, and with it, there is a bewildering variety of magic tricks possible.

Those who witness a magician doing card magic invariably attribute to him superlative manipulative dexterity. While this is sometimes true, usually he is credited with far more dexterity than he really merits, and it is his showmanship that is really laudable. There are countless effects possible that require no more than the knowledge of how to work them, plus the ability to 'put it over', and that, of course, is where showmanship comes in (of which more later).

In the pages which follow, there will be found tricks with cards which fall into this category, so that virtually no skill is required. However, the science of expert card conjuring has progressed and changed immensely in latter years, and there are hundreds of sleights that *could* be brought into use to enable the conjurer to present really baffling card miracles. Indeed, there are many followers of magic who make the study of card sleight-of-hand their whole time hobby, and become specialists in this branch of magic. It is not suggested therefore, that sleights with cards should be despised, and undoubtedly the study and practice of these sleights will prove more than invaluable. There are, of course, innumerable books on this subject, and the reader is invited to consult the Bibliography at the end of the book.

As in other hobbies, arts, or professions, certain words which are not in normal usage have come to be part of a common conjuring parlance, and at certain times throughout the book these words or phrases are used. For instance in the 'Card in the Orange' trick on page 14, reference is made to the word 'force'. This word when applicable to magic signifies that it is necessary for the performer to control the choice of a spectator. The latter does not realize this and is under the impression that his selection is not engineered in any way, whereas in actual fact the conjuror by subtle means, has 'forced' his choice. In order to make sure everything is understandable a complete glossary will be found at the end of the book listing such words and phrases, giving definitions and even reference when necessary.


## THE MILLION TO ONE MYSTERY

Although this pleasant little card mystery is perhaps, misnamed, its effect on the audience certainly lives up to the title. All that is required is a pack of cards, which the performer fans so that a spectator may select one. This is done, and the audience remembers the card selected. The performer does not know the identity of the card which is now returned to the pack.

The spectator then deals out the entire pack into two piles, one face up and one face down; at the same time he is asked to note if his selected card falls into the face up pile. It is apparently in the face down heap - so this is also dealt into two piles, again one face up and the other face down. Yet again the selected card does not show amongst the face up cards. This is continued until but one card is left, and this is seen to be the *selected card*.

This is a practically self-working trick, and the only preparation necessary is to trim carefully any card along the top edge so that it is a fraction shorter than the rest (*1B*). This is known as a SHORT CARD and is used as a key card or locator card. Incidentally, this particular principle will be found useful in many effects. Place the

SHORT CARD in a position 22nd from the top of the pack - now you are all set to go!

Fan the cards so that the spectator is able to choose one freely. While he is looking at it, square up the pack and riffle through the cards until you locate the short card. (*See illustration 1A.*) Divide the cards at this point and have the selected card returned above the short card; this will bring it to a position 22nd down from the top of the pack.

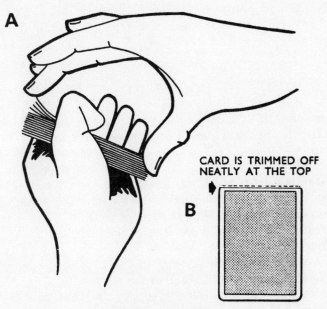

*Figure* 1, A *and* B

A point to watch when having the card selected, is to try to ensure that the card is taken from the part of the pack below the short card. If, however, the chooser insists on one above, it does not matter although you must see that when it is returned to the pack, it goes, into the 22nd position. Naturally the short card will help you to do this knowing that it was in the 22nd position to start with, and with the selected card removed it has become the 21st.

The trick is now done as far as you are concerned. All that is necessary is to instruct the spectator to deal out the cards into two heaps, one face up and the other face down,

commencing with the face up pile, and they are dealt
alternatively on each pile. The selected card will always
fall into the face down heap, so this pile is picked up
again and dealt as before, the first card face up, the
second card face down, and so on. This is continued until
the last card remains.

Have the spectator name his card and then get him to
turn over the remaining card in his hand - and it will be
seen that this is the selected card.

NOTE.- Some people may prefer to use a thick card (*See*
page 154) as a locator card; the trick can then be done
impromptu.


## DO AS I DO

This is one of the most baffling of all card tricks -
especially so because the action takes place mostly in the
spectator's hands. Two genuine packs are needed. They
can, in fact be borrowed, so it makes this particular feat
ideally suitable for working *impromptu*.

The spectator and the performer each take a pack, the
spectator being given the choice of either. They shuffle
their respective packs, then each exchange their packs with
the other.

The spectator is then asked to think of any one of the
cards in the pack - the magician does likewise.

Now each looks for his mentally selected card in the
pack he is holding - removes it so that only he can see its
face.

The whole point is that only the spectator and the
magician know the actual cards which are removed, but
the performer does not know what the spectator's card is
and the spectator likewise is unaware of the performer's
card.

These cards are placed on top of the respective packs.
The packs are now cut several times, the remembered card
being hopelessly lost. In this condition the packs are
exchanged.

They each look for their card in the pack and place it
face down in front of them.

8

Simultaneously they each turn their card face up. When the faces are visible it is seen that each card is *identical*.

## Method and presentation

After the packs are produced, and while they are being shuffled, the performer notes the bottom card of his pack. That is the very simple secret, but here is the actual presentation in easy stages.

1. The two packs are produced.

2. Spectator selects one pack - magician picks up the other.

3. Each shuffles his pack, the magician secretly noting the bottom card of his pack.

4. After shuffling the packs, they are exchanged.

5. Each mentally selects a card. (The magician merely remembers the previously noted bottom card for convenience.)

6. Each removes his card from the pack, gazes at it for a moment and then places it on top of the pack.

7. Each then cuts his pack and completes the cut. This can be repeated several times.

8. The packs are now exchanged.

9. Each looks for his card in the pack and removes it. (The performer actually looks for the noted bottom card and removes THE ONE ABOVE IT. The cards are now held face up, remember?)

10. Each lays his card face down on the table, and when they are turned face up, they are seen to be identical.

If you have followed the moves, you will readily see that when the cards are exchanged, you know the identity of the bottom card and the spectator is unknowingly induced to place his mentally selected card next to it.

You do not know his card until you get the pack back into your possession again, but you *do* know what card is next to it, and that is how you are able to take out the same card as he, proving that 'two people can think of the same card at the same time.'

At least, that is exactly what it seems like to the audience!

9

# THE REVELATION CARD TRICK

This is an ideal drawing room trick and although a slight amount of preparation is necessary, the ultimate effect is well worth while.

Here is what it looks like to the audience. Several spectators are asked to select a card, and each having remembered the identity of their own card, returns it to the pack. They then, each in turn, call out the name of their chosen card, while the performer writes them down on separate slips of paper. These slips are folded and placed on a plate. Now someone steps forward and selects one of the slips; the rest are burnt.

The card written on the selected slip is called out, and the performer takes the ashes from the burnt slips and rubs some on his forearm. To everyone's amazement, the name of the selected card appears in black letters on the arm.

*Figure 2*

To accomplish this quite spectacular trick it is necessary to prepare your arm beforehand.

Using a piece of wet soap, print the name of the card on your arm; when dry the letters will be invisible.

How do you know the name of the card? Easy! It is the same as the short card used in the first trick ('The Million to One Mystery') let us assume that the short card is the Jack of Clubs.

Now for the selection. Riffle through the pack and have someone call 'stop'. The spectator is handed the card stopped at. Do this several times, each person taking their card, but see that one of the spectators 'selects' the short Jack of Clubs. It is a fairly simple matter to coincide stopping at the short card just as the spectator calls 'stop'. See also page 15 for the further description of this 'force'.

Have your slips and a pencil ready, and when the different cards are called out, begin to write them down, but here's the trickery – you write down the same card every time – the Jack of Clubs! This is unsuspected by the audience of course. All that remains to be done now is to have a slip selected, and the remainder burnt. This destroys the evidence.

When the card is called out, merely rub the ashes on to the soaped arm, and the letters will stand out boldly (*See 2*).

Try it!

NOTE – The paper upon which the names are written should be of a light quality and easily combustible; this saves time during the presentation.


## THE SEVEN MYSTERY

The Seven Mystery is a card trick with possibilities of a splendid patter story culminating in a surprise finish. It should be presented as a table trick, possibly after a game of cards. The performer leads in the conversation with a reference to the 'mystic quality of the figure seven'. 'There are seven days in the week, seven wonders in the world, and so on. Demonstrating that 4 and 3 make 7, the top seven cards of the pack are arranged in the form of a seven face down on the table. (*See 3*.)

Someone is now asked to point to any card in the vertical row which forms the upright of the figure seven; this being done the remaining three are placed with the balance of the pack.

One of the row of three is next turned over and its value is noted, and the cards to that value are dealt from the pack on to it face down. For example, if it was the eight of Hearts, eight cards are placed on it. If it was a

11

picture card such as the Jack, eleven cards are similarly dealt.

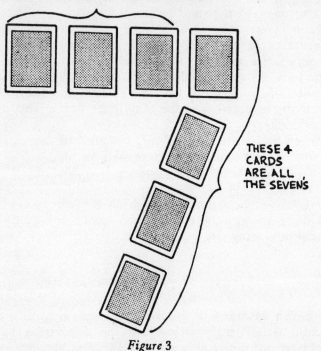

THESE 3 ARE INDIFFERENT CARDS

THESE 4 CARDS ARE ALL THE SEVENS

*Figure* 3

The next face down card of the line of three is turned over, and again its value in cards is dealt on top. Finally the last face down card is turned face up, and its value in cards is placed on this. (*See 4.*) Reminding the spectators of the importance of the figure seven, the solitary card originally in the line of four is turned over and it is seen to be - a seven! Whereupon, remarking that it would be a coincidence if any of the others turned out to be a seven, all the face down heaps are turned over and the bottom cards of each are seen to be sevens.

METHOD - Begin by having the four sevens together on top of the pack, this being unknown to the audience. Lay the top seven cards to form a figure seven, the four sevens being positioned first to form the upright part (*Refer again to 3*).

The top row being completed with any cards, next have one card of the vertical row of four selected, the remaining three being dealt with as follows.

*Figure* 4

The pack which has meanwhile been held face down in the left hand is dropped on to one of the sevens. The whole pack is picked up again and dropped on to another seven, meanwhile the other hand picks up the remaining unselected seven and places it on the top of the pack. The actual selected seven is left remaining face down on the table. This manoeuvre will result in there being two sevens on the bottom of the pack and one seven on the top.

But while this has been going on, you have directed attention to the remaining row of three cards. One of these is turned over and its requisite value in cards is dealt from the top of the pack face down on to it as in 4. Then direct someone else to turn over any of the other two face down cards.

While they do this, quietly move the bottom card of the pack which is a seven and place it on top.

Deal off the value in cards on to the second face-up card as before.

Finally have the last of the three turned over, meanwhile moving the bottom card of the pack to the top as before.

Everything is ready for the finale; the selected card is now turned over to reveal that it is in fact, a seven. Then all the face down heaps are turned over, and the rest of the sevens are seen to be the bottom cards of these heaps.

NOTE - If you wish, the sevens can be shifted from the bottom of the pack to the top while executing a shuffle. It will be found however that ample misdirection will be provided while the spectator turns the card face up.

## THE CARD IN THE ORANGE

This is an outstanding feat of card magic and can be performed in the parlour, yet is equally suitable for presentation before a large audience on a stage.

The effect is briefly this - the performer has a card selected from the pack, which is torn into pieces; one identifying piece is kept by a spectator, the remainder disappears and the selected card is found inside an orange, fully restored, except for the corner; and the missing corner is found to be the piece kept by the spectator, which fits the restored card exactly.

You will need the following 'props' for this effect. Three oranges, a pack of cards with an additional extra card, this pack also to contain a short card. A double envelope easily made by sticking two envelopes back to back (5A).

Tear a corner from the duplicate card and place it in one side of the double envelope (5B).

The remainder of the card is now rolled as tightly as possible and inserted in the orange. This will make a convenient cavity for the rolled card. Gently push this into the fruit, being careful not to break the peel around the stalk part. Now stick the stalk back in place with glue or rubber cement; the orange will then appear quite ordinary, and will withstand examination.

Place the duplicate of the card in the orange above a short card, about the middle of the pack. (See 'Million to one Mystery', regarding the short card, on page 6.)

Arrange all your props on the table; see that the faked orange goes in the centre of the three. It is a good plan to balance these on three glass tumblers. Oranges usually have different natural markings on them - make sure that you can identify your faked one quite easily.

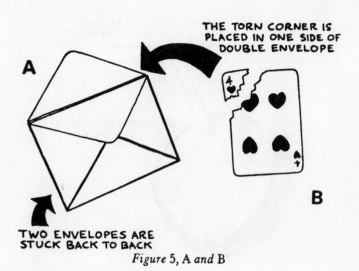

A

THE TORN CORNER IS
PLACED IN ONE SIDE OF
DOUBLE ENVELOPE

B

TWO ENVELOPES ARE
STUCK BACK TO BACK

*Figure 5, A and B*

You are now set to perform.

Begin by riffling the cards; ask a spectator to call stop, however, do not stop but actually continue riffling very quickly to stop at the short card. Cut the pack at this point and have someone take the bottom card of the upper half - this will be the 'force' card, of course. But remember that the impression you try to convey with this type of force is that you stopped when commanded by the spectator and that the extra riffle you gave should be done speedily and pass unnoticed. The selected card is now torn into pieces by a spectator and while this is being done, you pick up the envelope and secretly steal out the small piece already there. The envelope is offered open so that the spectator may drop the torn pieces into it. Make as if to seal the envelope, but as an afterthought say - 'you had better keep one piece for identification'. Saying this, reach with the finger and thumb into the envelope which secretly holds the small piece. Pretend to remove any piece, in reality you allow the concealed piece to come into view. This is handed to a spectator for later identification.

Seal the envelope and place it in a position so that all

may see it. Refer now to the oranges and ask someone to select one.

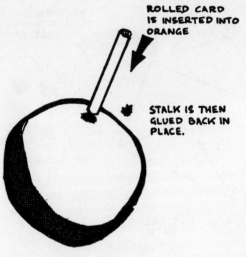

**ROLLED CARD IS INSERTED INTO ORANGE**

**STALK IS THEN GLUED BACK IN PLACE.**

*Figure* 6

If he selects the centre one, give it to him, throwing the other two away into the audience. If he selects one of the others throw this out to the audience. This will leave two, one of which contains the card. Have him make another choice. If he selects the fake, give it to him, throwing the other to the audience. If he selects the other orange, throw this out to the audience leaving him with the fake. This is known as the 'conjuror's choice'.

You now pick up the envelope and with it, gesture to the orange, saying, 'That is the one you want?' As you do this, turn over the envelope, rip it open showing that the blank side is empty, and that all the pieces have disappeared. The orange is now peeled and broken open, and inside is found the selected card, minus the corner. The corner which is in the audience is found to fit perfectly.

Instead of using the double envelope the pieces may be burnt if desired.

In this case, use an ordinary envelope and have the pieces dropped in, the whole lot, envelope as well, being destroyed. Naturally, any force card can be used and two further simple but practical and efficient forces will be found at the end of the chapter.

See page 113, the trick referred to as 'Burnt and Restored Paper Money'. For a variation of this trick. The card could be found and restored in a borrowed cigarette instead of the orange.

## THE RISING CARDS

The Rising Card Trick is one of the most famous of all card effects; it is visible magic at its best, and well worth featuring in any act. There are many ways to perform this marvellous feat, some of them require expert sleight of hand while other methods involve the use of intricate mechanism. The method about to be described is not difficult to do, yet does not require any particularly complicated apparatus. First, let us deal with the effect as it is seen by the audience. The conjuror cuts a pack into two piles, and having done so a pile is selected and three cards are removed from this part, their values being remembered. It is well to note at this point, that the three cards are genuinely and freely selected. After being noted they are returned to the other part of the pack in any position.

The two half packs are then placed together, and inserted into the card case, this is held with the fingertips, and slowly a card is seen to rise out of the pack; it is seen to be the first selected card.

The other two cards also rise out of the pack in a similar fashion, and they too are seen to be the actual, selected cards.

Well, that is exactly what the audience see, and no one can fail to agree that it is really a marvellous effect. Like many of the best tricks, however, this is also very simple, and a few minutes spent preparing the pack will make it ready to work.

Secure a very sharp knife and cut a rectangular hole in twenty-six of the cards. (*See 7, A and B*). This should be just big enough to allow your index finger to be inserted into it.

Now carefully prise up the card which is normally glued to the back of the card case, and cut a rectangular hole in the case to correspond with the hole in the cards. Press back the card so that the hole is out of sight. To set up the trick, stack the whole pack face down as follows, 25 ordinary cards, then the 26 fake cards on the top of these and lastly place an unprepared card on the top of the pack; replace them in the case.

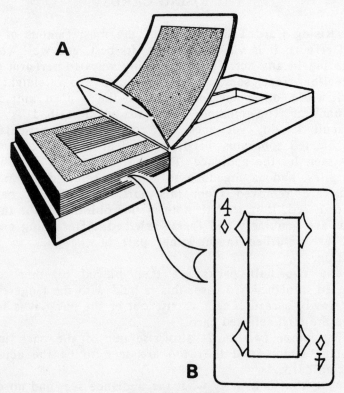

*Figure* 7, A *and* B

TO PRESENT - Remove the whole pack from the case and give them a false shuffle (*See page 22*). You must leave them with the pack order undisturbed. Now carefully cut the pack in two, and have someone point to one of the heaps. Do what is known as the conjuror's choice; if they select the genuine half, allow them to take it. If they select the fake half, you pick it up and tell them to take the remaining half.

Three cards are now removed from the unfaked half, these are noted and returned anywhere in the faked half you are now holding.

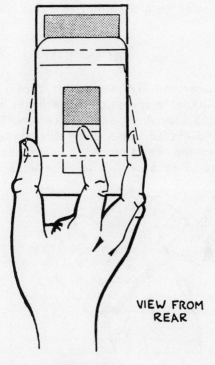

VIEW FROM REAR

*Figure* 8

This half is then dropped on to the remainder of the cards and the whole pack is turned face up. The bottom card (it was previously the top unfaked one) is now openly removed and inserted into the pack (see that it goes into the unfaked part).

Without showing the backs, replace the whole pack in the case.

Stand well back and hold the case in an upright position, thumb on one side of the case and fingers on the other. Use only the second, third and fourth fingers to support the case, the forefinger is free to work the rise (*See 8*).

Insert this finger under this flap, and into the hole. Press upwards against the card, which will be one of those selected. The card will rise, and eventually it can be removed by a spectator.

Do the same with the other two selected cards.

## ACES OUT

The performer shuffles a pack of cards, holds them face down and invites a spectator to push out a packet of cards with a match (*See 9, A and B*). This packet is completely removed and placed aside. The same procedure is repeated three times, and when the four heaps are turned over the bottom card of each heap is seen to be an Ace.

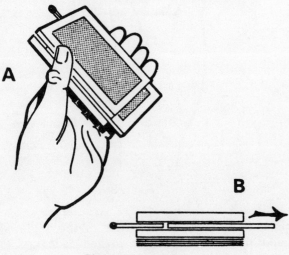

*Figure* 9, A *and* B

'Aces Out' is a very good prelude to 'The Four Ace Trick' which follows and is accomplished very simply.

The prior preparation consists of secretly removing the four Aces and having them in readiness on the bottom of the pack. The pack is placed in the card case in readiness for the trick.

To PRESENT - Remove the cards, and holding them with the backs to the audience, shuffle them so that the bottom stack of four cards is not disturbed. This is very simple to do and is effected whilst executing what is known as 'The Overhand False Shuffle,' (see end of this trick for the full description).

The cards are now held face down in the left hand. Using a match the spectator pushes the little packet of cards from anywhere in the centre of the pack towards the rear. Grip the protruding packet with the fingers of the right hand - fingers on the top with the thumb going beneath (*See 10*). Apparently remove the whole packet and place it to one side, but as the thumb reaches under the packet, it also slides the bottom card of the pack (one of the Aces) and brings this out, secretly adding it to the bottom of the packet.

This done four times, when the heaps are turned over all the Aces will be seen, one on each of the withdrawn piles.

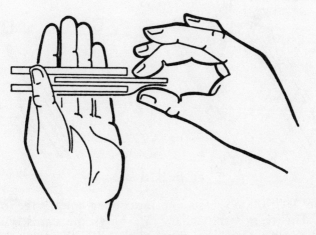

*Figure* 10

Actually this particular shuffle, being easy to do, is the one in most common usage for other tricks, and will enable you to keep the bottom (or top) part of the pack in position whilst apparently giving the pack a genuine shuffle.

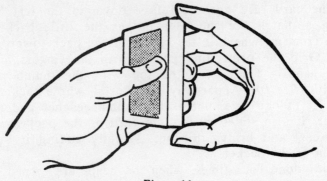

*Figure* 11

Hold the cards as shown in 11, just as in the normal position for shuffling. The back of the cards facing towards the left. (The illustration shows the view as seen by the performer.)

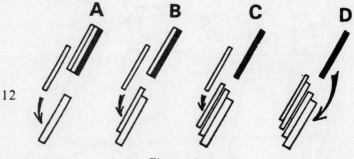

*Figure* 12, A *to* D

The left thumb rests on the upper long edge of the cards. The right hand meanwhile holds the cards with the thumb against the near short side, with the right fingers resting against the far short side. The left thumb slides a few cards off, (*12A*) whilst the right hand carries the balance of the cards upwards and over the cards in the left hand, and then allows a few of these cards to drop from the top of this packet on to those held in the left hand (*12B*).

The left thumb again slides a few more cards from the top of the right hand packet and deposits them on top of the left hand packet (*12C*). The right hand meanwhile keeps a firm grip on the bottom few cards and finally places them *beneath* the cards in the left hand (*12D*). This manoeuvre enables you apparently to shuffle the pack leaving the bottom few cards in their original position just as they were before the shuffle.

If you wish to keep the *top* part undisturbed it is only necessary to ensure having the face of the cards facing left at the commencement.

It will be seen that any small quantity previously stacked in a specific order on the top or bottom of the pack will remain undisturbed, yet you have apparently given the pack a fair shuffle. Although it has taken many words to describe, the whole operation takes only a short time to execute, and being deceptive as it is, it is well worth practising. Follow the text with the pack in hand.


## THE FAMOUS FOUR ACE TRICK

If you have already introduced the trick described on page 20 called 'Aces Out', in the climax you will have four Aces in full view on the table - failing this, the Aces are openly removed from the pack.

You ask someone to turn them all face down on the table, meanwhile you pick up the balance of the pack, and while all attention is centred on the Aces, you take the opportunity to reverse secretly one half of the pack, so that the other half faces inwards. You now have someone pick up any three Aces in turn and hand them to you. The pack should be held in the left hand, and taking these Aces you place them all face down on top.

Now refer to the remaining Ace and ask someone to turn it face up. Meanwhile your left hand casually drops to your side and you secretly turn over the pack in your hand so that the Aces are now at the bottom. When the cards are again brought into view, however, the audience will not suspect this because of your little subterfuge. Assuming that the Ace remaining on the table was the Ace of Spades, you lay the top three cards side by side face down saying, 'and these are the Aces of Clubs, Diamonds and Hearts.' You are still holding the pack in the left hand, and as you reach over to turn the Ace of Spades face down on the table, your arm effectively masks the pack from view, and at this instant you turn the pack over once more. The Aces will now be on top. Say that you will now deal three ordinary cards on each Ace, you deal the three top cards (Aces) first on to the Ace of Spades, the next three on the next card and so on.

The position is now as follows: there are four piles of four cards face down on the table. The audience think that the bottom card of each pile is an Ace, whereas in actual fact they are all in the first heap. This heap is picked up and placed in the breast pocket, the cards still in view.

The remaining three heaps are gathered together and cut, then given to a spectator to hold in a firm grip. The final *denouement* now takes place. You cause the three Aces to leave the cards held by the spectator, to change places with three indifferent cards in your pocket. Show that the cards from your top pocket are now indeed all Aces, and when the spectator examines his cards he finds all the Aces to have vanished, he being left with only indifferent cards.


## CLEOPATRA'S NEEDLE

A playing card is selected from the pack and after being noted it is returned and the pack is wrapped in a sheet of newspaper.

A large bodkin on which is threaded a length of coloured ribbon is now thrust through the packet by a spectator, and the ribbon is held at both ends with the packet suspended in the centre.

The performer now breaks away the paper and removes the cards. When the remaining paper is torn away the

24

actual selected card is seen on the ribbon, having been penetrated by the needle.

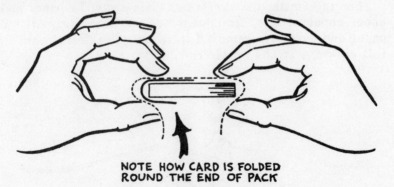

NOTE HOW CARD IS FOLDED
ROUND THE END OF PACK

*Figure* 13

METHOD - The paper, needle and ribbon are unprepared but there is one short card in the pack (*See page 6*). The bodkin is actually a very large carpet needle about 6 in. long and a highly coloured ribbon about 6 feet long is threaded on to it. Have the short card on the bottom of the pack.

PRESENTATION - The cards are fanned for a spectator to remove a card. After it has been withdrawn, cut the pack in two parts and have the card returned on to the top of the upper part of the pack. The bottom half is now placed on top of this. The spectators think that the card is now buried and lost in the pack. Actually the short card being above, you can locate it quite easily.

Give the pack a false shuffle (*See page 22*) or a series of cuts and finish by cutting at the short card thereby bringing the selected card to the top.

Proceed to wrap the pack in newspaper, but as soon as the cards are out of sight, push forward the top card so that it projects over and round the short edge of the pack (*See 13*).

Note that in this illustration, the paper is shown by the dotted line, and of course a much larger piece is used in order to wrap the pack completely.

This packet is now held for a spectator to insert the needle. It penetrates the card and the ribbon is pulled completely through, the ends now being held by two spectators.

For the finish, the performer tears away the paper and under cover of this, straightens out the bent card. All the paper and cards are removed to reveal the selected card in full view and strung on the ribbon (*14*).

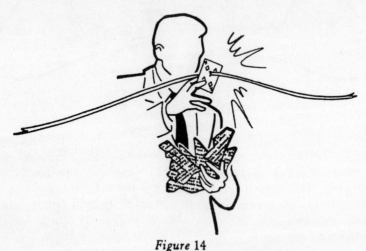

*Figure* 14

## THE CONCLAVE OF KINGS

Secretly place the four Kings face down on the top of the pack.

Hand the pack to a spectator and ask him to cut the pack into four equal heaps. These are placed side by side - be sure that the heap containing the Kings goes to the extreme right. Now have him pick up the left hand heap and from it deal three cards face down on to the place they just occupied and then to continue by dealing one card on to each of the four piles. The balance of the cards should be put to one side.

He is further instructed to pick up heap No. 2 (second from the left) and likewise deal three cards into the blank space, followed by one card on each pile. Heap number three is dealt with similarly, and also heap number four (this being the extreme right hand heap). Now tell him to turn over the top card of each pile - he will be surprised to discover they are all Kings.

NOTE - The normal procedure adopted by almost all people when cutting the pack into several heaps is to grasp the bulk of the cards and leave the bottom part in the original position, then placing the remainder to its right again leaving another section on the table, repeating this move with third and fourth heap. If this is not done, however, it is a very easy matter to arrange the stacks to suit yourself in a pretence that you are going to mix the piles up.

## AN EASY FORCE

Place the card that you wish to force on top of the pack; you can shuffle the pack now, but see that the top card remains undisturbed. See page 22 for a description of this shuffle.

Ask a spectator to cut the pack into two piles. He is then asked to indicate any pile. If he selects the top half of the pack (the force card is the top card of this section) ask him to turn over these cards and place them crosswise on the remaining half (*See 15*). Now have him turn over all the cards. You briefly recapitulate what has happened. Then ask him to look at the top card of the face down pack - it will of course be the force card.

TOP CARD OF THIS PART IS THE FORCE CARD.

*Figure* 15

If, on the other hand, he indicates the bottom half of the pack ask him to place this pack crosswise on the other heap. Again you take his mind from what has taken place by recounting what has happened, saying, 'Let's have a

27

look at the card where you cut'; he is told to note the top card of the bottom pile - it will be the force card.

So you see, that in any event, he is made to 'select' your force card. It is surprising how this simple ruse fools people, and the spectator invariably thinks that the card came out of the centre of the pack, where it was cut to, in fact.

Ah, well!

## ANOTHER CARD FORCE

This is possibly one of the easiest of all 'forces' - a most convincing one, too. Begin by having the card to be forced on top of the pack, and have the bottom card secretly reversed so that it is face upwards.

Hold the cards in the left hand, then spread a handkerchief over them; as soon as they are covered however, secretly turn over the whole pack, and have a spectator cut the cards through the handkerchief (*See 16*). As he does so, you reverse the part of the pack remaining in the left hand under the handkerchief, and bring it into view, then have some one look at the top card of this part. It will be the force card.

The spectator will naturally think that he cut at this point and he will not suspect that you controlled his choice in any way.

If the handkerchief is opaque enough to prevent the bottom card showing through, you need not resort to the subterfuge of reversing the bottom card at the commencement.

The illustration shows the spectator's hand indicated by 'S' cutting the pack. The performer's hand is not shown but of course it reverses the lower part of the pack under cover of the handkerchief before it is brought into view again.

You can just as easily force more than one card using this method.

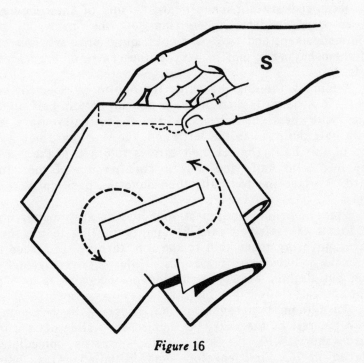

*Figure* 16

## THE PHOENIX CARD

Just like the legendary bird called the Phoenix, this card becomes restored from the ashes.

A spectator selects a card, notes it and returns it to the pack which is cut several times in order to lose the card. Placing the pack behind his back the performer successfully locates the selected card.

It is now signed and placed inside an envelope which the spectator himself retains for safe keeping. Another envelope is shown empty, sealed and also marked for later identification.

Envelope No. 1, containing the signed, selected card is now burnt together with its contents. Some of the ashes are dropped over envelope No. 2 which is torn open and to everybody's surprise the original signed selected card is extracted from it.

29

Required are a pack of cards - one of these being a short card which is on top of the pack at the commencement and two envelopes, quite ordinary, but one of them having a spot of wax at the centre of the address side.

Begin by fanning the cards for one to be selected, and while it is being looked at, strip out the bottom half of the pack with the right fingers and thumb, so that you are left with half the pack in the left hand, the short card being on top of this half. The selected card is returned to the top of the left hand half, and thus it goes on top of the short card. Replace the top half, then have the pack cut several times.

Place it behind your back and it is an easy matter now to locate the selected card by simply riffling to the short card and bring them both to the top, turning them face up with the selected card uppermost. Holding them together as one but slightly offset on the top of the pack as in 17A. The spectator now signs his card.

Turn them both over as one, squaring them together with the rest of the pack, but immediately slide off the top card (short) with the left thumb - this is immediately placed in the first envelope and initialled. After being shown empty the second envelope is rested on top of the pack which is used as a solid writing surface whilst the spectator signs it.

This envelope is now placed in a prominent position but due to the wax, it carries away with it the selected card (17B). Envelope No. 1 is destroyed; your hands being obviously empty, pick up the second envelope. Tear off the top, reach down inside it and appear to take out the card. Actually your fingers go inside the envelope, thumb outside, and the illusion of withdrawing it is perfect (18).

Pass the card around for verification that it is indeed the original signed, selected card.

NOTE - Those who are adept at using the pass and the double-lift will realize that the use of the short card can be dispensed with.

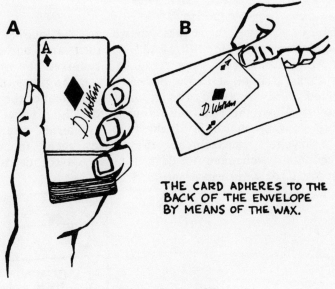

A

B

THE CARD ADHERES TO THE
BACK OF THE ENVELOPE
BY MEANS OF THE WAX.

*Figure* 17, A *and* B

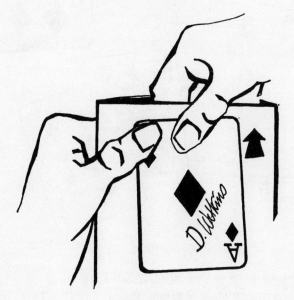

*Figure* 18

# JOKERO

EFFECT - Five cards are shown to the audience - someone is asked to MENTALLY select any one. The performer turns them face down and removes one of the five cards, placing it in his pocket. When the name of the selected card is asked for it is found to be the one removed. Now, the remaining four cards which have been in full view on the table all the time, are turned over and to everyone's amazement they are seen to have unaccountably changed to four Jokers. All the cards are passed out for rigid examination.

*Figure* 19, A *and* B

APPARATUS - (a) A special fake card, one side of which shows four different faces (*19A*). This is easily made by glueing three different cards on the face of one other card. (b) Four ordinary cards which are the duplicates of the four ordinary cards shown on the fake (*19B*). (c) Five Joker cards.

SET-UP - Place three Jokers face up in the left hand and on top of these place the fake card, face up: finally place another Joker face up also. Keep this group of cards secure with an elastic band. Now place the remaining five cards in your pocket in a memorized order.

You will notice that the fake cards in 19 read from the top down, Clubs, Hearts, Spades, Diamonds and it is advisable to use any similar group of four cards of four different suits because they can easily be remembered by the word 'CHASED'.

PRESENTATION - Remove the banded set of cards from your pocket and holding them face down in your left hand, count them separately showing them as five single cards. Replace them in the same order back in the left hand still face down.

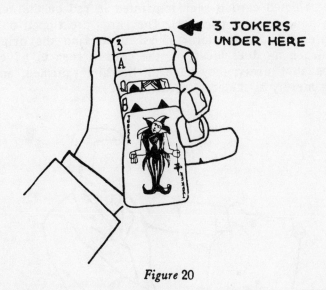

3 JOKERS
UNDER HERE

*Figure* 20

Turn them face up - now pull down the top face card, (Joker) so that it reveals the five different cards holding them stepped up in your left hand as shown in 20. Hold them in front of the spectator asking him to MENTALLY select any card and remember it. Close up the cards and

33

turn them face down. Now deal them in a row face down on the table. Pick up the fake card and drop it in your pocket. For the first time ask the spectator to name his card. When he does so, remove that card from among the genuine ones already in your pocket.

As the final payoff, turn over all the remaining cards on the table and they will be seen to be all Jokers and, of course, they can be passed for rigid examination.

## SHOT AWAY CARD TRICK

A card is selected, noted and returned to the pack which is replaced back in its case.

A handkerchief is wrapped round the case and held by a spectator. Now a toy miniature pistol is introduced and fired at the pack. When the case in unwrapped, a facsimile of the selected card is seen imprinted in red on the centre of the handkerchief (*See 21*). The cards are tipped out of the case and the spectator is asked to find the original card. When he does locate it, the card is seen to have all its pips 'shot' away; they have all literally vanished, and it is now merely a 'skeleton' card (*See 22*).

*Figure* 21

Apart from the small toy pistol which is only used to give a dramatic effect, you will need to prepare the following props. First the handkerchief. An ordinary white gentleman's handkerchief is used. Lay it over the four of Diamonds so that the pips show through the fabric. Using a red ballpoint pen, carefully trace and fill in the four pips plus the two small ones and also the figures. You will now have a perfect imprint of the card on the handkerchief, this will wash out in time but the colour can be renewed when necessary. It is best to 'print' the card diagonally on the hanky as shown in 21.

*Figure* 22

Now for the skeleton card. Taking a duplicate four of Diamonds and using a sharp knife, carefully cut out all the six pips, leaving holes in their place.

Finally you will need a special card box, which although easily made, is a most ingenious idea for causing a card to vanish. Carefully peel away the sample card which is usually stuck on the back of the box. Now cut a small window in the bottom half of the box as shown in 23. This aperture is then covered with a small piece of Contact Impact plastic, with the tacky side inwards. (Sellotape will work just as well, but the other seems to stay tacky longer.) Stick the card back on the box, and it will now seem quite innocent of preparation.

Set up the pack by having the skeleton card on top and immediately under this the duplicate four of Diamonds. Put the pack in the case pressing slightly over the window causing the skeleton to adhere to the inside back of the box. Fold over the side corners of the hanky in order to hide the imprint then fold in half and tuck it into the top pocket.

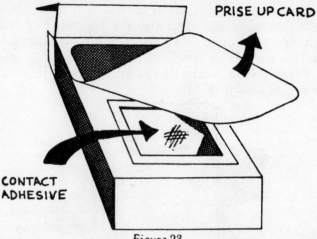

PRISE UP CARD

CONTACT ADHESIVE

*Figure* 23

In working the effect, you tip the cards out of the box, but of course the skeleton card will remain stuck inside unsuspected by the audience, so lay the case casually aside at this point. The top card of the pack is the genuine four of Diamonds. Ask someone to name any low number, we will suppose that the eight is called, so deal off eight cards from the top of the pack. But, as if an afterthought, replace them back on the pack again. This places the four of Diamonds in the eighth position from the top. Say to a spectator, 'you had better do the counting'. He counts to the eighth card and notes that it is the four of Diamonds. It is returned to the pack but brought to the top, the deck being replaced back into the case. As you do so, however, pull the skeleton card forward with the finger-tip so that it enters the middle of the pack. Press slightly on the window to make the genuine four of Diamonds now stick to the inside.

Take out your handkerchief and without revealing the imprint wrap it round the box.

Fire the pistol, a spectator unwraps the box and to

everyone's surprise the imprint of the card is seen on the handkerchief. Tip the pack out of its case (the genuine four of Diamonds stays stuck inside). When the spectator searches through the cards, he finds the four of Diamonds with all the pips 'shot' away.

## CARD SET-UP

Arrange the whole pack as follows: the first half of the pack, all Kings, tens, eights, sevens, fours and aces (24 cards). They can be in any order. The second half of the pack should comprise all the Queens, Jacks, nines, sixes, fives, threes and twos (28 cards). The latter figures all have 'hooks'; for instance, the curly part of the 2 and 6 is an obvious 'fishhook'.

If a card were to be selected from one section of the pack to be replaced anywhere in the other section, it can easily be detected. For example, a spectator selects, say, the eight of Hearts, memorizes the card and replaces it in the pack. See that it goes in the other section. You will now be able to fan through the pack and immediately tell which was selected because the 8 stands out among the hooks. There are many tricks possible with this set-up, and no doubt many ideas will present themselves to you.

In the foregoing card trick it will be found advisable to use cards which have a white border on the back design. Most packs are like this, however; but if you use a design which takes the colour right to the edge in an all-over pattern, it will be difficult to execute the reverse moves such as those used in the 'Four Ace Trick' and 'Card Force'.

---

# CHAPTER 2 - CLOSE-UP MAGIC

The performance of magic 'close-up' has had a wave of popularity among conjurors during the past few years - and for a good reason - it is fast becoming an important branch of conjuring. Despite the general belief to the contrary, performing tricks close up is no harder than performing them on the stage, indeed in many cases one is able to resort to many ruses which are of no use except when one is working right next to the audience.

The beauty of doing tricks right under people's noses is that they give you greater credit for doing them thus. It is also very satisfying to be able to entertain your friends at a moment's notice and you will gain tremendous popularity. In any case it is as well to be a magician off the stage as well as on!

It only takes one other person to make an audience and it is always great fun to do apparent miracles with borrowed articles, and if a few likely props are always carried with you, there need never be a dull moment for your friends when you are around.

Doing tricks close up provides you with plenty of practice and assists you in overcoming the difficulties appertaining to each trick; thus will be engendered within you the confidence needed to perform before larger audiences. All the top-line conjurors of today - and those of the past - have gained great fame merely because they had a trick 'up their sleeve' ready to present when the occasion arose.

Almost everyone you meet will know at least one trick or stunt, and when they know that you are a magician they will invariably try it out on you. This is where you can perhaps add to your store of magic tricks, but do not despise the catches, gags or stunts that are so often shown: these are usually great fun. So much fun in fact can be gained by working these stunts or gags that a special section at the end of this chapter is devoted to them - all are quite practical and are easy to do. Remember your prime aim is always to entertain, and if you can memorize a few of this type of thing too, your own repertoire will be increased and your reputation will be enhanced.

The tricks described in the following pages are really very simple, but care should be taken when showing them, just as in all branches of magic. Some of them are true classics and if you take the trouble to practise them well, your growing fame as a wonder worker may entitle you to take your place among the great ones in magic, even though the tricks be small.

## COIN IN THE BOXES

To those not 'in the know' this trick can be one of the most baffling. A coin is borrowed (for later identification) and then inexplicably disappears, to be found later, inside a little cloth bag. This is inside a box, and this box is also inside one another, the whole being inside a larger one. All the boxes are securely wrapped with elastic bands. The spectator himself removes the boxes, and the coin really is the one that was borrowed and marked.

Although there is little preparation prior to the trick I think you will agree that it is well worth while. First of all you will need a tin tube, which is never seen by audience, yet as a matter of fact is the part that really does the job. - Incidentally, any piece of apparatus used by a conjuror but unsuspected or unseen by the audience, is called a 'gimmick'.

The tube is constructed from a piece of sheet tin or aluminium about 2 in. x 2 in. and the short sides are bent inwards to form a flat tube about  in. wide and 2 in. long. These are rough dimensions but in any event it should be of such a size that a dime can slide through unimpeded (*See 24A*). Now make a little cloth bag about 2 in. x 1 in., to be placed on the end of the tube and securely fastened with an elastic band (*See 24B*).

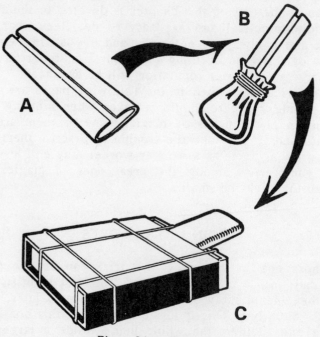

*Figure* 24, A, B *and* C

Place the bag end of the tube in a matchbox, again wrapping elastic bands around both ways (*See 24C*). Procure another box big enough to take the matchbox and treat this the same way. If you so desire a further box may be used. Always secure well with rubber bands, and contrive to leave a good portion of the tube protruding. Place the prepared box into the outside left hand jacket pocket and you are then all set.

Obtain a wage type envelope and drop into it a dime. Now paint a glue line down the centre inside the envelope, forming two compartments, then along the top, sealing the coin into one of the compartments.

Neatly slit open the bottom of the section that does not contain the coin. The diagram should make this clear (*See 25A*).

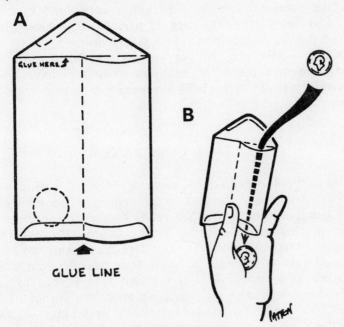

*Figure* 25, A *and* B

To PRESENT — Borrow a dime and have it well marked with a knife, and holding the envelope in the left hand, the bottom being against the palm (*as shown in 25B*), openly drop the coin inside. As you seal the flap allow the coin to drop out into the left palm. Fold the envelope into three so that the bottom is in the centre, and in this condition is given to someone to hold. The coin can still be felt inside the envelope. Meanwhile the left hand casually and unhurriedly drops to the pocket, and the coin is inserted into the tube, thus travelling into the bag, after which the tube is withdrawn from the boxes.

The sealed boxes are now openly taken from the pocket and placed in full view.

Attention is directed to the envelope which the spectator is still holding. He assures everyone that the coin is still there because he can still feel it; you take the envelope from him and tear it into little pieces, placing them aside, the inference being that the coin has vanished.

Have someone remove the rubber bands and take out each box until the little bag is arrived at; when this is opened the marked coin is found safely inside.

NOTE - Be sure to get rid of the faked coin still among the torn pieces of envelope. You will have ample opportunity to do this whilst everyone's attention is on the boxes.


## ANOTHER COIN VANISH

Another simple method to cause a coin to vanish is as follows. Previously insert a small coin into the hem of a large handkerchief, and when ready to perform, pretend to wrap up the borrowed coin in the hanky. However you secretly palm the coin in the left hand and give the wrapped coin to someone to hold. They feel the coin which is in the hem, thinking it is the one they loaned to you. Make the coin vanish by whipping away the corner of the hanky, shaking it out. Show the hanky both sides and then reproduce the original coin in any manner you wish.


## PINS 'N BEADS

Simple props are used in this effective divination effect. You show three large safety pins on each of which has been threaded a different coloured bead.

Someone hands you one of these pins behind your back, hiding the other two - you are immediately able to tell him what colour the bead is.

Look at 26 and you will see how it is done. One pin

has the point blunted (easily done with a file) the second pin has the point slightly curled over (do this with pliers) while the third pin is left normal. They are shown exaggerated in the drawing to illustrate the points.

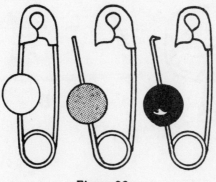

*Figure* 26

When the pin is presented to you behind your back you secretly open it - feel its point which will immediately tell you the colour of the bead. You have of course memorized which is which.

Coloured ribbons tied round the pins will serve instead of beads.


## THE MAGIC NAPKIN RING

A napkin ring is covered with a playing card and then placed over a borrowed coin. When the card is removed it is seen that the coin has vanished. The card is replaced, and the napkin ring removed, to reveal the coin once more. This is an improved version of what is known as 'The Harness Ring Trick' and really a very old effect. Good though it was, however, it had one drawback - the ring could not be passed for examination. In the method described here, the ring, card and coin can all be passed for inspection and will undoubtedly fool even the knowing ones!

Obtain a thin but stiff piece of cardboard; from it cut a

43

circle which will fit tightly into a napkin ring. Push this down to the bottom to form as if it were a box with no top (*27A shows ring and fake*). The remainder of the cardboard is squared off and used as a sort of table mat.

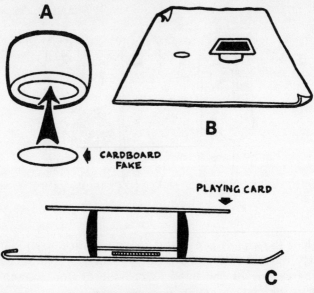

*Figure* 27, A, B *and* C

Before you begin, the ring stands on the 'cardboard mat', the fake being at the bottom. The playing card is handy. It will be seen that if one looks into the napkin ring, the fake, which shows, will be taken for the cardboard mat showing through the bottom of the ring.

PRESENTATION - Borrow the coin and place it on the mat. Show the ring but do not lift it up. Now place the playing card on top and lifting both together place the ring over the coin.

When the ring is uncovered the coin will have disappeared. Again cover with the playing card and lift the ring clear thus revealing the coin once more.

Ask the spectator to examine the coin, meanwhile you pick up the ring and card, pressing the fake bottom up and against the playing card, carrying this fake away under cover of the card, and then pass round the ring for inspection. While the mat is also being scrutinized take the opportunity to push the faked circle into your hand out of sight.

The playing card can now be passed out.

If you do not want to palm the fake piece, place the card and the fake together in your top pocket, but with the card protruding. If need be when the card is eventually given for inspection the fake is left behind in the pocket.

27B shows the card on the ring but with the coin not yet covered and still in view.

27C shows a section-view of the set-up when the coin is covered.

## CORD RESTORATION

This restoration of a piece of cord or string is ideal for working very close up.

The performer first of all shows two pieces of cord tied together at the ends. A spectator is asked to select one of the knots. He unties this, while the performer unties the other.

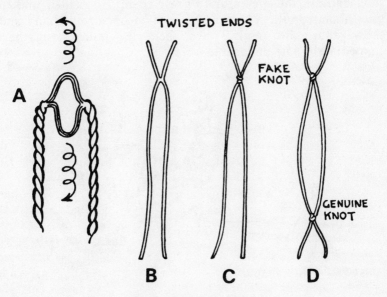

*Figure* 28, A, B *and* C

The two ends held by the performer now weld themselves together in a most mystifying fashion, and the cord is passed round for inspection, no trace of any join being visible.

The type of string to use is thick two-ply sisal or two-ply rug wool, but it must be two-ply or a string which has an even number of strands.

Using a piece about two feet long, double it in half and where the centre comes, separate half the strands from the other half (*28A*) twisting each half together to give the appearance of two ends as in 28B.

Tie these two ends into a knot (*28C*) and this gives the appearance of two pieces of cord tied together. Tie the other genuine ends in a similar fashion (*28D*). You are now ready to present the trick.

Show the cord and have someone point to any knot. If they point to the genuine one ask them to untie it while you untie the fake one. If the fake one was pointed to you say, 'Right. I will untie it while you untie the other.' This you do, and still concealing the fake, but now untied, ends in your hand (*29*), you let one end protrude from each side, and ask the spectator to grasp them. He is then told to give a sharp pull. You will be able to open your hand and show that the ends have become joined together. Immediately pass round the cord for inspection.

*Figure* 29

# MATCH BACK

The magician shows a book-type packet of matches and carefully counts the number of matches it contains. One of them is now removed and the packet given to someone for safe keeping. The match is ignited and completely burnt, the ashes being sprinkled over the booklet from whence it came. When it is opened the match has apparently been 'restored' and has found its way back into the folder again.

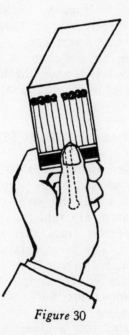

*Figure* 30

An ordinary booklet of matches is used but it is best to have only about eight or nine matches for ease of counting. As you open the packet for the matches to be counted, secretly turn one of them down and conceal it by the left thumb, as shown in 30. The matches can be openly counted, then one removed. Close down the cover with the right fingers but, as you do so, turn the booklet back uppermost with the left fingers. The bent-down match is then folded neatly back into its place and you have shown the booklet on all sides to be free of deception.

Give it to someone to hold. The match is struck and completely burnt (or, if you prefer, make it disappear by palming it).

The booklet is opened and the matches counted - there are seen to be exactly the same number as at the commencement, the match is back with its fellows again.

Although the above effect is quite impromptu, with just a little preparation beforehand you can make the trick even more puzzling. Simply strike any one of the matches WITHOUT removing it from the booklet. The burnt match is the one that is secretly turned down. After the matches have been counted, any match can be removed, the 'folder is closed and given to someone to hold. The match is struck, then destroyed and when the booklet is opened the burnt match has found its way back into the booklet again.

## *PASSE PASSE* CIGARETTE PAPERS

A cigarette paper is rolled into a little ball and given to someone to hold. A second paper is torn into pieces which are also formed into a ball and given to another spectator.

When the spectators are told to unroll their respective papers, the first person finds that his whole piece has become little pieces, and the spectator who held the torn pieces discovers that his pieces have become restored to a whole piece. The trick is very simple to do and being, as it were, performed under the very noses of the audience, makes an ideal close-up 'routine'.

Before you begin, roll a cigarette paper into a little pellet and have it in some easily accessible position. A good plan is to keep several pellets in the ticket pocket of your jacket, so that they are ready for a performance of the trick at any time.

Hand the cigarette paper packet to someone and have him remove a paper; you meanwhile take the opportunity to secure the rolled pellet. This is held between fingertip and thumb of the right hand out of sight (*See 31*).

Take back the paper from the spectator between the same finger and thumb, and tear it in halves and halves again and so on until only small pieces remain. Roll the pieces into a ball and continue the rolling motion, substituting the whole piece for the torn pieces.

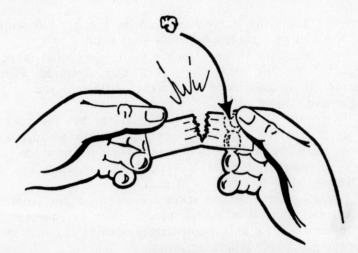

*Figure* 31 *Illustration shows pellet concealed and paper being torn. View as seen by performer*

Hold the two pellets together as one and show all round that your hands are otherwise empty. Ask a spectator to grasp the switched pellet between his fingers and thumb. You are now left with the torn pieces.

Remove another cigarette paper, roll this into a pellet and, executing the same switch, give the other (torn pieces) pellet to the second spectator.

The trick is now finished as far as you are concerned, but you now apparently cause the respective papers to change places; when the holders open their papers they will see that the change has taken place.

NOTE - The switch is the most important move in the above effect, and it literally takes place before people's eyes The actual exchange is effected in the act of kneading the chosen paper into a ball, and almost instantly the prepared pellet is handed to a spectator to hold.

# TORN AND RESTORED CIGARETTE PAPER

This makes an ideal trick to follow the preceding one because the two effects can be blended into one complete routine.

When doing the *Passe Passe* routine you are left with a whole pellet of cigarette paper in your hand.

It is necessary to have such a pellet concealed in your hand before you start the 'Torn and Restored Paper' routine. It is concealed as before, between your right finger and thumb.

There are several stages in this trick, but the general effect is that the cigarette paper appears to be torn into pieces and restored. The performer offers to show how this trick is done, but after a very 'lucid' explanation, the audience is left just as wise as ever.

*Stage 1*. The magician takes a cigarette paper from the packet and tears it into little pieces. Then he squeezes the pieces into a little ball, immediately opening it out to show that the pieces have been restored.

METHOD - After the paper is torn up, it is rolled into a ball and the switch is made, as in the *Passe Passe* routine, then the switched whole paper is opened up and shown.

At this point, having displayed the opened cigarette paper, roll it into a little ball and apparently drop it on the floor or in an ash tray, as if disposing of it. What really happens however is that the old master-move (switch) is put into operation again and the whole piece is retained in the fingers, in reality the torn pieces being disposed of. This leaves you with a whole cigarette paper pellet ready for the next stage.

*Stage 2*. Magician now offers to show how it was done, explaining that a duplicate was substituted for the torn pieces. A new cigarette paper is torn from the packet and rolled into a ball, this is openly placed between the fingers. Now another paper is removed and the audience see this torn up, carefully substituting it for the rolled-up piece which is then opened out to show that the pieces have been restored.

All this is made obvious to the spectators and they think they now know the secret. But the performer states that the difficult part of the trick is to dispose of the torn pieces of paper, and if you know the secret password 'hocus pocus' these pieces become restored too.

The pieces are opened out to reveal them as one whole piece, completely taking them by surprise.

At the finish of *Stage 1*, you are left with a complete 'balled-up' cigarette paper, but you say that a duplicate piece is needed, and this one is removed from the packet, rolled into a ball and placed between finger and thumb. This is done openly, but of course the spectators do not realize that a pellet is already concealed, and that these are held together as one.

The cigarette paper is then torn up and screwed into a ball and placed between the finger and thumb. All this you explain to the spectators, doing it as you speak. The position now is that you have two whole pellets and one torn-up pellet, all of them being held together as two pellets, and indicated as such to the audience. One of the whole pellets is opened out to show the paper restored.

They are all held in the left hand as in 31, on page 49 (*Passe Passe* routine), but the *extra* whole pellet is concealed from the audience. They think that the trick is now ended, but you roll the opened-out piece into a ball, rolling with it the torn pieces and allowing the whole pellet to take their place. Drop the rolled-up whole piece and rolled torn pieces on the floor. This leaves you with the supposedly still torn pieces, which you now open out to show that it is restored.

The routine described above will probably sound complicated but in practice it is quite simple to perform. The only subterfuges to master are the switch and the holding of the two pellets together as if they were one.


## THE MIGRATORY MONEY ROUTINE

This routine is well worth learning because it appears absolutely impromptu and is done with borrowed money. The only necessity is an extra bill which is rolled up into a ball and left in an easily accessible position ready for use in the second part of the routine. To make it easier to

51

follow, the sequence is divided into three parts, but even if they were used separately each section is an excellent trick in itself. The first part is called...

## (1) THE PUZZLING COUNT

Begin by borrowing three bills and have each of these screwed into a ball. Lay them in a row on the table in front of you, then pick them up, one at a time, counting 'one, two, three', as you do so. Then lay them down singly, counting 'four, five, six'. Pick up one, count it as 'seven'. Touch the next ball; push it aside, call it 'eight' and the next, push it aside also calling it 'nine'. Finally laying the last one down in your hand calling it 'ten'.

The balls are gathered up by you and placed into the spectator's hand, who is asked to count them as you did.

You will find that he will be unable to duplicate your counting, so you show him again; usually he will fail many times. The secret is to start the spectator off on the wrong foot, as it were. You always gather the balls up at the end of the count and dump them in his hand, saying 'Now you do it', and he will invariably begin by counting the first ball on to the table and so on.

It will not work this way, and though sometimes he may stumble on the secret by accident, if you again gather them up and place them in his hands, saying 'Good show, try again', he will probably be unable to repeat his success.

## (2) THE CAVORTING NOTE

This is where your extra balled-up bill comes into use and, at the end of the 'Puzzling Count', you should secretly obtain it and hold it in the right hand by the second, third, and fourth fingers against the palm (*32A*). The other three balls are on the table in a row.

Pick up the first ball between the finger and thumb of the right hand and give it to a spectator. Now pick up the second ball and have him do the same as you do. Tell him to place the ball into his left hand (you do this with your ball while he copies you). Now tell him to open his left hand and place the ball in his right hand. This he does and

52

you do the same, but what he does not see is that you have added this ball to the one already concealed there. Hold these two balls together as one (*32B*) and place them (he thinks there is only one) into his right hand together with the one he already holds there.

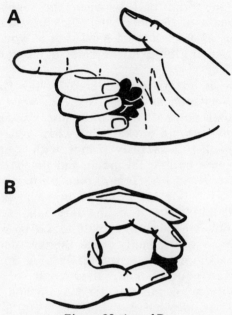

*Figure* 32, A *and* B

The position now is that he holds three balls but thinks there are only two. All you have to do is to place the remaining ball into the top corner of your trouser pocket so that when the lining is pulled out, the ball will remain hidden there. Then pull out the pocket - empty! The spectator sees that the ball has vanished and when he opens out his hand, he will find to his utter surprise that the missing ball has arrived there with the other two.

NOTE - For those who prefer to cause the balled bill to vanish by other means, a detailed description of an excellent vanish will be found at the end of this routine, on page 55.

## (3) BANKER

The preceding routine will leave you with a balled-up bill in your pocket. Secretly secure this and hold it as before in the right hand, and you are all set to work the next stage.

Pick up the first ball between the right finger and thumb and put it in the left hand. Pick up the second ball, and place this also in the left hand, but as you do so allow the *extra* ball being held in the right palm to drop in with it.

The move is adequately covered by the fingers. Close the left hand as soon as the balls are dumped into it. This leaves one ball on the table; pick this up with the right hand, place it in your pocket. But when your hand comes out of the pocket it secretly brings with it this last ball. Still holding this ball in the palm, tap the back of the left hand with the right forefinger, then allow the three balls to drop out on to the table. Offer to do it again. Pick up the first ball and place it in the left hand as before, but this time allow the concealed ball to go in with it. Show your right hand quite empty, pick up the second ball and push it in the closed left fist. Finally pick up the last ball and place it in your pocket. It is again secretly brought out. Tap the back of the left hand again and let the three balls tumble out once more.

Next time the move is varied.

Still holding the concealed ball in the right hand, pick up one of the balls between the left finger and thumb and pass it into the right fist. Repeat with the next ball, placing this in the right fist. Lastly the ball left remaining is openly placed into the pocket with the left hand and this time is left there. Bring the hand out showing it empty. Open the right hand to show three balls in this hand once more.

The bills can then be unwrapped and passed back to their lenders. Your own duplicate bill resides safely in your pocket.

Naturally it is just as practical to perform the foregoing with balled up pieces of paper instead of money — but somehow the use of bills creates a better psychological impact. These routines could just as easily be performed with small sponge rubber balls which can be made by cutting them from a regular bath sponge and trimming to shape with scissors.

## AN EASY VANISH

There will be many occasions when it will be necessary to make a small object vanish, and any time spent perfecting the following sleight will be found well worth while. This is called the 'Tourniquet Vanish' and if practised many times before a mirror something very near perfection can be attained. The sleight is very illusive and absolutely ideal for making any small objects, such as coins, balls, thimbles and so on, disappear.

Hold a ball between the fingers and thumb of the left hand (*See 33*).

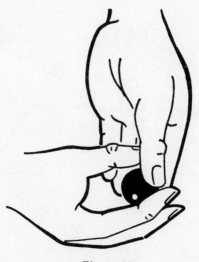

*Figure* 33

The right hand approaches the left, and appears to take the ball, the thumb going beneath, the fingers on top. As the right fingers close over the ball, let it drop into the left hand. The right hand moves away as if holding the ball, and the left hand drops casually to the side, the ball being held in this hand, loosely, by the fingers against the palm. Meanwhile all attention is misdirected to the right hand which simulates holding the ball, and this is caused to vanish by crumbling the fingers in a 'dissolving' motion finally showing this hand empty. It is important to misdirect the audience's attention by concentrating *your* gaze on the hand which you want them to look at, and by doing this, you will cause them to look in this direction as well.

## SUBTLE COIN VANISH

A coin is seen to be held at the fingertips and is covered with a handkerchief; when the latter is 'whipped' away the coin has completely vanished.

*Figure* 34

Hold the coin between the finger and thumb of the left hand (*See 34*). The back of the hand is away from you and should be held about a foot in front of the top breast pocket. The right hand holding the corner of the handkerchief draws it over the coin from the front, and as if to prove that the coin is still there, is drawn completely over and away to reveal it still in position.

The same move is repeated, but as soon as the right fingers pass over the coin they secretly grip it through the folds and, as the right hand comes level with the top breast pocket, you secretly drop it in the pocket while the handkerchief still apparently covers the coin. Then the handkerchief can be whipped away, to demonstrate that the coin has 'dissolved into thin air'.

Misdirect the audience's attention away from your right hand by gazing steadfastly at the coin in the left hand - the spectators will then also concentrate on this point.

## SPOOF COIN VANISH

The following coin vanish is very useful if you happen accidentally to drop a coin, when you are causing it to vanish by any other means.

Reach down and pick it up, but as the hand passes the trouser turn-up, the coin is secretly dropped therein. Continue to straighten up, the hand still simulating retention of the coin. Eventually cause it to disappear by rubbing the fingers - 'crumbling it away'. Do not forget to retrieve the coin from the trouser turn-up later!

Some people will find it easier to drop it into the shoe just below the ankle.

## HOPPITY MATCHES

This is an amusing little stunt which, if pulled off successfully, leads people to think that you have a good deal more dexterity than you may in fact possess! It also has the merit of being quite impromptu. You begin by borrowing four matches; now hold your hands in front of you, your palms uppermost, then ask someone to place one match in each hand. Close your fingers over the matches and ask a spectator to lay each of the other two matches on the fingertips, (*See 35*).

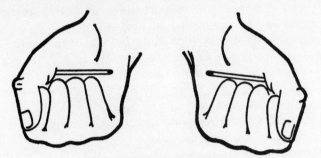

*Figure* 35

You now say that you are holding two matches in each hand, but you are going to cause one match to leave one hand and fly over to the other.

The hands are now turned over quickly, and when they are inspected sure enough there are three matches in one hand and one match in the other. It seems very clever, but is so easy to do when you know how.

Begin by having the matches placed as described, quickly turn the hands over, but in doing so, allow two matches from one hand to fall to the table, while the other hand opens and closes quickly allowing the match outside the fingers to join the one held in the fist. All this must be done quite quickly and imperceptibly while the hands are being turned over.

Still keeping the hands closed, you tell the audience that the matches slipped the first time, but you will attempt to do it again. The spectator picks up the two fallen matches and places them on the fingertips as before.

Again the hands are turned over rapidly, this time both are opened and closed allowing the matches to be secured. When eventually the hands are opened the audience do in fact see that in one hand there are three matches and in the other hand only one. Seemingly one match has mysteriously passed from one hand to another.

One of the oldest fair-ground or carnival tricks is called 'Pricking The Garter'. It is really an out-and-out swindle, because it is virtually impossible for the operator to lose! The trick as it was practised years ago involved the use of a leather garter, which in those days was long enough to wrap around the leg several times. A belt or even a piece of ribbon now serves equally well.

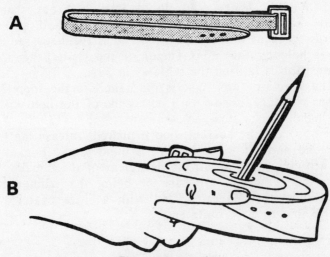

*Figure* 36, A *and* B

After the trickster had gathered a goodly crowd around him, he would proceed to demonstrate the effect. The strap was rolled up very neatly and laid on the table. The audience were invited to insert a peg into the centre of the the roll. If the operator is able to pull the strap free from the peg, the dupe loses his bet. If, on the other hand, when the ends were pulled the centre remained caught by the peg, the operator had to pay out. The whole point about this is that the performer can pull the strap clear, or can have it caught at the centre of the peg, just whenever he so desires. The result is always under his control and not subject to chance as he leads them to think.

A modern-day version can be presented as a table trick

and can in fact be done quite impromptu using a belt or similar strip of material and a pencil.

PRESENTATION - Begin by doubling the belt in half. Now roll it up neatly and place it on the table. Hand the pencil to a spectator and have him insert it into the centre loop so that when the belt is withdrawn it will be caught.

He does this quite successfully, but now challenge him to do it again. This time he does not succeed; indeed no matter how many times he tries to attempt it, he will always fail.

SECRET - When you double the belt see that the buckle side is a little longer (*See 36A*) and roll this towards the centre until the plain end is reached (*See 36B*). This is held by the index finger of the right hand and in this position is laid on the table as in 37A.

The spectator now inserts the pencil in the loop. If he guesses wrongly, simply pull both ends of the belt with the right hand.

If however the correct loop is picked, release the tip of plain end and allow it to swing around to the buckle end. You are now able to pull the belt clear of the pencil.

In this way you are sure of being the winner every time. Study the diagrams, and with a little practice you will be able to do it quite easily.

*Figure* 37, A *and* B

# THIMBLE VANISH

A thimble held on the forefinger suddenly disappears, to be produced eventually from the back of the neck. Two thimbles are needed and one is prepared by drilling a small hole in the side near the base. Thread a piece of black cord elastic through this. On the other end of the elastic fasten a small safety pin (*See 38A*). Pin the fake into the sleeve so that the thimble rests just out of sight but in an easily accessible position. The other duplicate thimble is secreted behind the neck in the collar.

TO PRESENT - Secure the fake thimble and place it on the forefinger. Display this - but do not reveal the elastic running up the sleeve (*See 38B*).

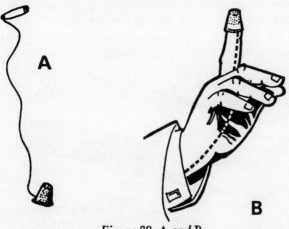

*Figure* 38, A *and* B

Bend the finger into your palm, at the same time releasing the thimble. This will fly up the sleeve and out of sight. Continue to hold the hand as if the thimble were still there, eventually 'tossing it in the air'. It disappears and you can then produce it from behind your collar.

# THE VANISHING MATCHES

A matchbox, inside which are a few matches, is shown and then closed. The box is then rattled to prove that they are still there, but when it is opened again the matches have vanished.

SECRET - A special faked box is required, easily made from an ordinary box. Obtain a box with a cardboard bottom, then a piece of paper the same colour as the inside of the box. (It may be necessary to completely re-line the box with paper.) The paper for the bottom is cut to exactly the width to fit inside, about an inch longer than the box. One end of the paper is glued to one end of the tray at the bottom, whilst the other is glued on the underside of the cover at the diagonally opposite corner.

The drawing will make this quite clear (*See below*). The paper strip should be of such a length that it will permit the tray to open to almost its full length, but to protrude no further.

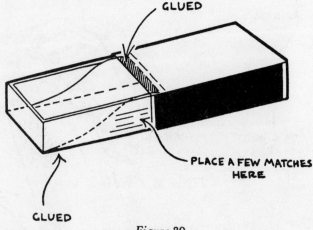

*Figure* 39

Open the box so that the true bottom of the tray shows and place a few matches in it. Close the box and push the tray out at the other end, where it will be seen that the glued strip hides the matches.

To present the trick you merely open the box to show the matches visible, close it again, rattle the box and open it at the other end to show that the matches have disappeared.

This device will serve equally well to vanish a coin instead of matches.

## THE EDUCATED MATCHBOX

The magician removes a matchbox from his pocket and places it on his hand, whereupon it proceeds to move forward in a most eerie fashion. Then to everyone's surprise it stands on end, when told to do so by the performer. To make the trick more baffling, the spectators see the box slowly opening, whence you extract a match.

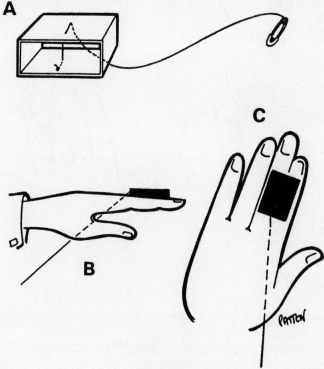

*Figure* 40

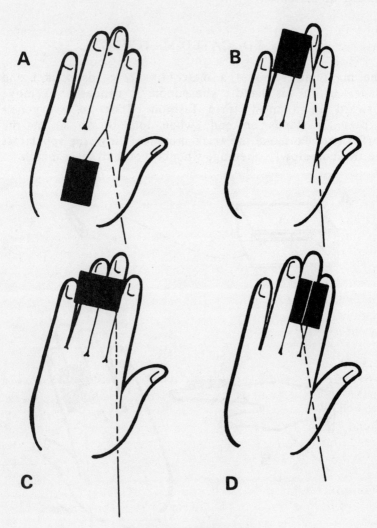

*Figure* 41, A, B, C *and* D

For close-up visible magic, the 'Educated Matchbox' is hard to beat. It can be carried around, as it is ready to work impromptu at any time. The beauty of the trick is that it can be performed quite close up.

SECRET - The matchbox is specially prepared. It is important that the matchbox used should have a tray that fits loosely, sliding in and out of the cover very easily.

Also required is a 24 in. length of very fine fishing line made of nylon. This is practically invisible at close quarters, but is immensely strong. In the absence of this, however, good strong, but fine black thread will suffice.

Before faking the box, remove the drawer. Now take the needle and thread it and pierce it through the cover at the centre about one-eighth of an inch away from the edge. Pierce it also through the exact opposite side of the cover. Then pierce it into the cover again one-eighth of an inch lower, letting the needle and thread drop right through the cover (*See 40*). The end of the thread on the top side should be tied in a knot and stuck down under the label, which is quite easily lifted. Remove the needle and replace at that end by a safety pin. Insert the drawer at the threaded end of the cover and push completely in. All that remains to do now is to attach the safety pin to the inside right-hand jacket and place also into that pocket the matchbox.

TO PERFORM - Remove the matchbox from the pocket; put it on the back of your hand so that the thread passes through the second and third fingers (*See 40, B and C*). Move the matchbox backwards its complete length. To make it move forward all that is necessary to do is to extend the hand and owing to the increased tension on the thread the matchbox will spookily travel its whole length. If further tension is now applied, the matchbox will stand up. Still further tension will cause the drawer to rise in the matchbox. You then, of course, remove a match or matches. Close the box and replace it in your pocket. It is always advisable to have a duplicate of this matchbox in your pocket, just in case someone may wish to examine it.

A further refinement is to have the drawer loaded at the end with a small piece of lead; the drawer can then be made to close at will.

With practice the 'Educated Matchbox' can be built into a really baffling, amusing and entertaining routine.

Position the matchbox as shown in 41A and move the hand forward to cause the box to creep towards the fingertips. Now place the box at the position as shown in 41B but with the thread hooked over the top right corner of the box. A slight movement forward with the hand will cause the box to roll over to the right.

Clip the matchbox lengthwise between the little and forefinger as in 41C. Move the hand forward to cause the tray to open to the left.

Close the box and replace on the hand but this time with the thread wrapped completely round as in 41D. You can now make the box do a complete somersault when the hand is moved forward.

## CHINK A LOOP

A piece of cord with a ring at each end is doubled and pushed through a small plastic or cardboard tube as shown in 42A. Then a pencil is pushed through the loop which now protrudes through the tube (*42B*). The rings are linked over the ends of the pencil (*43A*). Someone is asked to hold both ends of the pencil and everybody sees that the tube and cord are held secure (*43B*). A handkerchief is thrown over the pencil. Reaching underneath you extract the tube - it has apparently penetrated the cord. Everything is left with the spectators for a thorough examination.

The necessary props for this intriguing pocket effect are quite simply made.

(1) The cord is really made from a flat shoe lace, with small curtain rings sewn at each end.

(2) The tube is about 3 in. long by ¼ in. diameter - this could be made of cardboard, but an old fountain pen barrel cut to size would suit admirably.

(3) You will also require a special fake gimmick made as follows. Cut about an inch from another shoe lace and insert a small piece of plastic (collar bone) stiffening, sew or glue the ends with rubber cement.

(4) A handkerchief and a pencil, or thin stick complete the requirement.

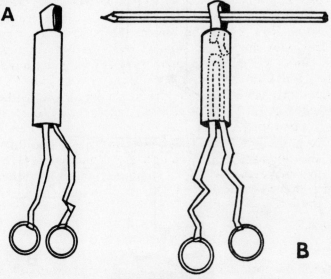

*Figure* 42, A *and* B

The only preparation needed is to place the small gimmick doubled over in one end of the tube, as in 44A.

To present the effect - introduce the tube, holding it with the gimmick end downwards. Show the cord and lay it over the top of the tube, with the rings hanging down equally on either side (*See 44B*). Holding the tube in the left hand with the pencil in the right push the cord down until the gimmick just protrudes at the other end (*See 45*). Turn the tube so the gimmick part is uppermost, then insert the pencil through the loop as shown in 42B.

Finally link the rings over the ends of the pencil, giving it to a spectator to hold both ends as in 43B.

Cover the pencil with the handkerchief, then reach beneath and take out the gimmick which will allow the tube to fall free. Palming the gimmick, whip away the handkerchief to show that the tube is now free. Dispose of the gimmick while the remainder of the props are being examined.

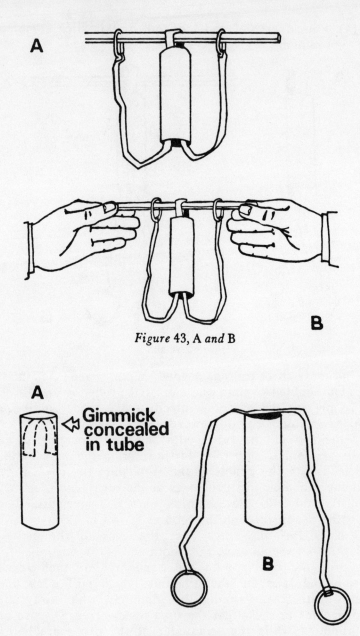

Figure 43, A and B

**Gimmick concealed in tube**

Figure 44, A and B

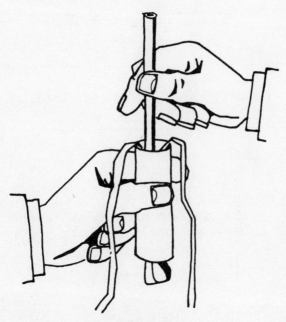

*Figure* 45

Incidentally it is a good presentation idea to use a chopstick in place of a pencil. The tube itself could be decorated with Chinese characters.

---

# CHAPTER 3 - STUNTS AND GAGS

Although they do not rank as conjuring tricks proper, the following stunts or gags are nevertheless interesting to the onlookers as well as being entertaining and sometimes amusing.

## THE NON-SHATTER BULB

Can you drop an electric light bulb onto a concrete floor from the height of four feet without breaking it? It's easy when you know how. Use an old bulb of course and hold it as shown in 46, with the metal adaptor part pointing towards the floor. Let the bulb drop and it will strike the floor without breaking.

*Figure* 46

## SMOKE WITHOUT FIRE

Peel a strip of striking paper from a safety match box. Set light to it on a metal ash tray.

Throw away the ashes and you will find a brown paste residue remaining in the ash tray.

TO PRESENT - Obtain a little of this paste on the fingertips and *by rubbing the thumb and fingertip together*, smoke will issue from them.

## MULTUM THROUGH PARVO

Take a small piece of paper about three inches square and place a dime beneath it, then mark out and cut a hole in the paper exactly the same size as the coin (*47*). Now challenge anyone to push a 50 cent piece through this hole, without tearing the paper.

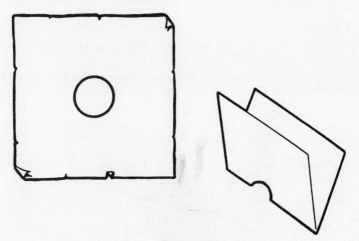

*Figure 47*

It is quite easily done. After your friends have given up, simply fold the paper in half, place the coin in the hole, slightly raise the top corners of the folded paper to open out the hole and you will find the coin will drop through without any trouble.

48 indicates exactly how it should be done.

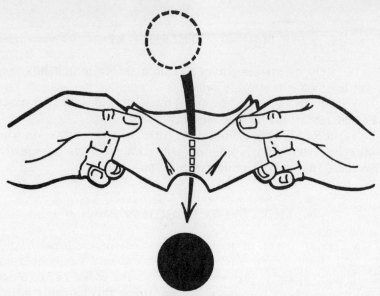

*Figure* 48

## THROUGH A HALF INCH HOLE

Another 'spoof' way to push a coin through a half-inch hole is amusingly accomplished by putting a pencil *through* the hole and pushing the coin. A cup or bottle can be pushed just as easily (*See 49*).

*Figure* 49

# BREAKING A PENCIL WITH A BANK-NOTE

After stating that you are able to break a pencil with a bank-note, you prove that it can be done. A pencil is bill, you prove that it can be done. A pencil is borrowed and someone is asked to hold it firmly as shown in 50.

The bill is folded in half lengthways and held at one end by the finger and thumb. Using it as one would a knife, it is brought sharply down onto the centre of the pencil.

Immediately the pencil is seen to be snapped cleanly in two.

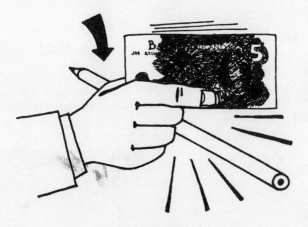

*Figure* 50

The secret is to extend your forefinger at the precise moment of impact with the pencil. It is the finger which breaks the pencil and not of course the bill. But you make great play of carefully creasing the bill so as to give a knife edge, and make one or two feints before you finally bring it briskly down on the pencil.

It is important to tell the spectator to hold the pencil absolutely firm between his two hands. Withdraw the finger as soon as the bill has passed through the two halves.

## COIN DIVINATION

Remove a handful of coins from your pocket and hold them behind your back while a friend selects one. He holds it tightly in his hand so that you cannot see the date. Pop the other coins back in the pocket.

Now write a date on a piece of paper. When the coin is inspected, the date is found to be the same.

All the coins in your pocket have the same date though they are of different denominations. Easy eh?

## BALANCING A GLASS ON A FIVE POUND NOTE

Can you balance a glass on a ten dollar bill? Sounds impossible doesn't it. It's quite easy when you know how. All you have to do is to fold the money so that it is corrugated as in 51. This gives it the strength to support the glass, which is balanced as shown.

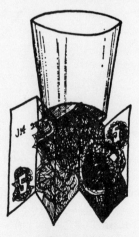

*Figure* 51

# TYING A CIGARETTE IN A KNOT

Can you tie a cigarette in a knot without breaking it? It's easy. Simply roll it in cellophane (take it from the outside wrapper of the cigarette packet) twist the ends securely as in 52, and you will find that the cigarette can be tied in a knot. When it is opened out, although a little bedraggled, it is still quite 'smokeable'.

*Figure* 52

# WINE FROM A CORKED BOTTLE

You can challenge your friend to drink a brandy from the bottle even though it is still securely corked. How? Turn the bottle upside down and fill the cavity with the liquid and you can now drink from the bottle as shown in 53.

*Figure* 53

# DEAD MATCHES

A spent match is picked out of the ashtray and the end is rubbed in the ash. To everyone's surprise it is struck on the box and ignites just like a new one.

Make a supply of fake matches by covering the head and burning the wood below it until it is just about to ignite. Extinguish the flame, dip the end in black ink and then in some ash. The match now looks just like a spent one.

Secretly leave it lying in the ashtray, and at a suitable moment casually pick it out, show it, then strike it.

# PREDICTO

Ask someone to write down a number comprising three different figures. Tell him to reverse these numbers and to subtract the smaller from the larger. If he tells you the first figure, you are immediately able to tell him the complete total.

For example if he thinks of 832 reverses to 238 and if he takes the smaller from the larger, the result will be 594. The sum will appear as in 54.

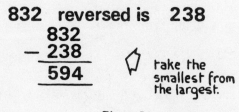

**832  reversed is  238**

$$832 - 238 = 594$$

take the smallest from the largest.

*Figure* 54

He tells you the first figure, which is 5, and you tell him the complete answer.

SECRET - The middle figure of the answer will *always* be 9. If you are told the first figure, which is 5 in this case, and you subtract this from 9, leaving 4, your complete answer is 594. This will work out every time; merely take the first figure which is given you from the 9, which is always in the middle, to give you the last figure.

## MAGIC PREDICTION

After trying the foregoing trick, you can then work the following stunt, which carries this principle one stage further.

Write on a piece of paper the figure 1089, fold up the paper and leave it on view, but with the figures hidden. Ask someone to think of three different figures as before, reverse them and subtract the smaller from the larger. Now have him reverse this total and finally add these together. When he finishes, show him your piece of paper.

His total will be the same as your prediction.

For example, assuming the first three figures selected were 865, reversed they will be 568. Taking the smaller from the larger will leave 297, this reversed will be 792. This added to 297 will give the total 1089; (*See 55*) for example.

```
   865   reversed & subtracted
 - 568
   297   answer reversed again
 - 792   then added
  1089   always gives this answer
```

*Figure* 55

Here is another trick with numbers, for those who delight in this pleasant form of mental recreation.

Ask someone to write down a large number composed of five or more digits, then to add these digits together and finally subtract the total thus obtained from the large number.

Now ask him to cross out any one of the digits in this total, then tell him to call out all the remaining digits, slowly one by one.

You can immediately tell him the number that was crossed out.

SECRET - When he calls out the digits, you mentally add them together, then subtract the total from the next largest multiple of nine and this will give you the figure marked out.

For example, if the total you mentally obtained was 21, the next largest multiple of nine will be 27, so 21 from 27 will give you six, and this would be the number which was marked out.

56 shows this example.

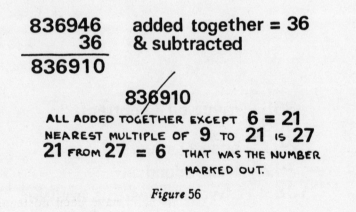

**836946**   **added together = 36**
**36**   **& subtracted**
**836910**

**836910**
ALL ADDED TOGETHER EXCEPT **6 = 21**
NEAREST MULTIPLE OF **9** TO **21** IS **27**
**21** FROM **27 = 6** THAT WAS THE NUMBER
MARKED OUT.

*Figure* 56

# CHAPTER 4 - MENTAL MAGIC

'Magic of the Mind' is rapidly gaining popularity as a form of entertainment. This new branch of the mystic art calls for a special presentation, your aim being to deceive the mind and not the eye. Whereas the ordinary conjuror openly displays skill in presenting his tricks, the 'Mentalist' tries to cover any sign of dexterity and endeavours to create the impression that his feats are accomplished by coincidence or by telepathy. Generally it is not wise to mix the presentation of mental effects with that of conjuring and mental magic should not be presented as tricks. Avoid also the use of unusual looking props; in other words keep away from magical apparatus as such. The mental effects that follow make use of very ordinary articles, the sort of things you would in fact use if you *could* read minds.

Tempting though it is, it is wise however not to sustain the belief that your mysteries are psychic; it is rather better for you to let your audience decide for themselves. If they say afterwards that there is no explanation for your tricks, it is comforting to know that you have mystified and entertained them. But if you lead them to think that you really do possess supernatural powers, you may have baffled them but your statement will have been misleading and untrue and of course not really fair. Psychology plays an important part in the presentation of mental effects; for instance if you write the figures one to ten in a row, and ask someone to cross out any figure, the chances are that the number seven will be crossed out nine times out of ten.

If you offer three articles for selection, usually the

centre object will be chosen, and if you ask a spectator to select a colour from, say, about six different coloured silk handkerchiefs, he will favour the red one on most occasions. Ask someone to name the first card that comes into their head, and you can gamble on it being an Ace or at least one of the Picture Cards, usually the King of Clubs.

If you set out to apply to mental magic the ground principles of magic which are outlined in this book, you really will baffle your audience. Remember the golden rules: keep your plot simple, use everyday articles as props if at all possible, try not to combine manipulative magic with mental effects and lastly have faith in the trick. Believe in it, and this impression will somehow be imparted to the audience as well, and although you do not actually say so, they think that you possess the key to wonderful powers not normally granted to ordinary people.

In mental magic as in all other branches of magic, there are a few tried and trusted principles on which many effects are based. One of these principles is known as the 'One ahead principle'. The following effect is an admirable example.


## TELEPATHY

A pack of cards being handy, someone selects a card and without revealing it, writes the name on a small piece of paper.

A second spectator is asked to write on another slip of paper the name of a film star. The third spectator writes the name of any town, the fourth, the name of a flower; several people in fact can be invited to write similar names on other slips.

These are folded into four and are dropped into the performer's cupped hands one by one.

The folded notes are now thoroughly mixed up, and one is eventually removed, while the others are dropped on to a plate. Without opening the note the performer holds it to his forehead and immediately tells the audience what is written on it. The person who wrote it is asked to verify that the information is correct. This note is screwed up and put aside. Another is taken, and again the performer reveals the contents, yet without opening it.

Once more the performer is correct, thus demonstrating that he apparently possesses telepathic powers.

So it goes on, until all the notes have been dealt with. They can of course be examined at the conclusion of the trick, and they will be found to be quite ordinary.

METHOD - All that is needed to present this trick is the ability to force a card, the rest is purely acting.

Firstly, have your cards, together with pencil and paper. You can borrow the latter if you so desire; merely fold the paper and tear off the notes to a convenient size, about 2½ in. x 1 in. is ideal. Have a plate or cup handy to act as a receptacle for the folded notes. Do not tell your audience what to expect, but begin by forcing a card (*See section on card tricks*). This must be done so that the spectator does not realise the card is already known to you.

The selector is told secretly to write the name of the card on his slip of paper.

You can, if you like, have another spectator cut off any number of cards and write the number he has cut on his slip - this gives you an adequate excuse to use the cards in the effect, but, as if to make it more varied, have people write such things as flowers, towns, colours, etc. on their slips.

Do not have too many, six is about right.

Now instruct them all to fold their slips in halves again so that the writing is hidden, then, commencing with the first spectator (the man who selected the card), they are all dropped into your cupped hands. Here there is a secret move. As soon as the first note is dropped in your hands, clip it between two fingers and in this way keep control of it while all the others are mixed around.

Holding your hands still cupped have someone reach in and extract any note. It will be easy to ensure that he does not get the 'card' note. As soon as this is done, drop all the other notes into the dish, releasing the 'card' note last. Note where it is in the dish and keep track of it all the while.

The spectator now hands you his selected folded note,

which you take, and holding it to your forehead in an attitude of concentration, you divine its contents. You pretend that on it is written the name of a card and, apparently after some difficulty, announce it (the forced card).

It will of course be verified by the person who wrote it. But as if to make sure yourself you open the slip and read it again pretending to call off the card. Do not let anyone see what is actually written on it and in this instant assimilate what actually is written on it; we will assume it is a town, say, Bradford. Screw up the paper and place it aside. Pick out another note and hold it to your forehead; this time you pretend to divine that on it is written the name of a town, Bradford. The writer will verify this is the town he thought of.

You open it out and confirm that it is indeed the town. Glimpse once more the information on this slip and then screw up and put aside.

Thus you are one ahead all the time.

Continue this procedure until all the slips are dealt with, and all the information has been 'divined' by you, and has been ascertained as correct. The last *billet* to be 'read' is of course the card *billet* - the one you have kept track of.

The *billets* themselves can be examined.

Providing that your acting and presentation has been well put over, this feat will be one of the most talked about after your performance.


## PSYCHOMETRY

The Mentalist hands a blank visiting card and an envelope to each of five different people.

They are all invited to write their initials on their cards and to place them in the envelope. The envelopes are gathered up by another spectator, who is asked to mix them up thoroughly.

No one can know which envelope contains which

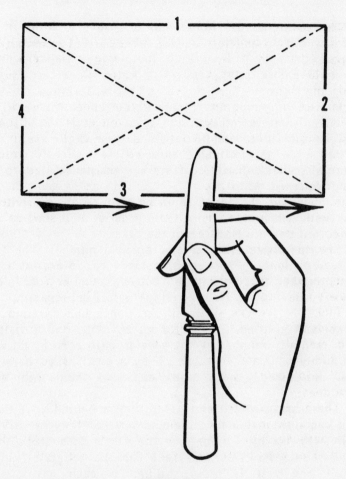

*Figure* 57

card, least of all the performer, who has not touched them since the beginning of the experiment.

These are all given to the performer who holds them behind his back. He produces them one by one and correctly divines which envelope belongs to each spectator. The cards and envelopes will withstand examination before and after the effect.

SECRET - Whilst there seems to be no explanation to this mystery, there *is* a subtle secret which is very little known even to experienced conjurors.

The envelopes are faked, but in such a way that their secret would go undetected even after careful examination. Prepare them as follows: Lay an envelope flap-down on the table and firmly press on a knife blade, running it along the bottom edge (*See 57*). This will flatten the two thicknesses of paper and create a fine edge which can be detected from the others. If the envelope is held lightly between the finger and thumb, and these digits are drawn off the edge, the untreated side will feel slightly bumpy, whereas the faked edge offers no resistance due to its being flattened out.

A fine sense of touch must be acquired to present the trick with confidence, but a little practice will soon enable you to tell one envelope from the other.

The envelopes are mentally given a number. The first is treated along its top edge, number two along its right edge, number three along the bottom, number four along the left side and the fifth envelope is left unprepared.

PRESENTATION - Break the paper band around the packet and give each spectator an envelope and a visiting card; mentally numbering the spectators to correspond with the number of the envelope. They are all asked to write their initials on their cards and seal them into their envelopes.

These are shuffled and given to you behind your back. You can now manoeuvre them to sense if they are all the right way up by feeling for the flaps; then stack them address side upwards and feel for the tell-tale 'knife-edge'. The rest is plain sailing; as each envelope is 'divined', hand it to the person concerned to verify that it does indeed contain the card with his initials on.


## COLOUR MYSTERY

The performer passes several coloured pencils or crayons for examination. They are all identical except that they are each a different colour.

A spectator is now asked to place one of the pencils into a glass tube whilst the performer's back is turned, the remaining pencils being hidden out of sight. The performer is handed this tube behind his back. He then instantly calls out the colour of the pencil. The trick can be repeated as often as you like; the pencils are quite ordinary and the tube is simply an aspirin phial or anything similar, the pencils being just big enough to go into the tube. Everything can be examined before and after the effect.

No doubt you are eager to know how this is done, and you will find that it is very simple indeed.

As soon as the tube with the pencil inside is handed to you, turn and face the audience still holding the tube behind you. Take off the cap and allow the pencil to protrude enough to enable you to scrape the lead or the crayon part with your right fingernail. This will leave a very small particle of coloured matter under your nail.

Replace the cap and as if to assist in your concentration you hold your forehead with your right hand. Steal a glimpse of the tell-tale fingernail and then reveal the colour whenever you like. The trick can be repeated several times.

A glass tube is suggested because they are more readily obtainable - but an opaque container can be more effective because this can be held against the forehead, the implication being that you are able to 'see' right through it and so divine the colour.

## THE PENCIL TELLS

Here is one effect that really savours of the 'unknown', and to the spectators there seems to be no possible explanation for it. This is exactly what happens. The performer tells everyone that he is going to attempt an effect which has a *touch* of the supernatural about it. he lays four different coloured pencils on the table and invites anyone to select one of them. The choice is absolutely free and the chooser may change his mind if he so desires.

Now a spectator is asked to think of any person who is dead. Then he is asked to remove a single leaf from a packet of cigarette papers, to examine it thoroughly and screw it into a ball. The ball is now impaled on the end of the pencil and the spectator is then asked to hold it in a very peculiar fashion. He is instructed to place his elbows on the table and hold the pencil between the forefingers and thumbs of each hand (*See 58*). The spirit of the departed person is then invoked. The pencil will be seen to waver slightly and eventually he is asked to remove the rolled-up paper, and on it is seen the name of the dead person written in the actual colour that had been selected.

The paper and pencils can be minutely examined.

The effect on the spectators when seeing the name on the paper is startling, and there are many who will be prepared to believe that it really is brought about by psychic powers. It is wise however to remind the spectators that they are witnessing a performance of *conjuring*, and what they see is accomplished by *physical*, and not *psychic* means.

*Figure* 58

Some little preparation is necessary to enable you to present this trick, but once the props have been secured it only takes a few seconds to prepare it for the next performance.

APPARATUS REQUIRED -

1. Four pencils (differently coloured), the points having been specially sharpened.

2. Packet of cigarette papers (although these can be borrowed).

3. Four special pencils about 2 inches long, the same colour as the genuine pencils. We will assume that the colours are RED, GREEN, BLUE, BLACK. The red pencil is sharpened at both ends, the green has a notch cut at the end, whilst the black one is unprepared. It will be seen that these different colours can now be identified by touch (*See 59*).

4. A special pocket writing-pad made by hinging two pieces of cardboard together, with a cigarette paper inserted and all fastened with a rubber band. The top piece of cardboard has a 'window' cut out of it (*See 60*).

WORKING - The small pencils and pocket writer are in the right hand trouser-pocket.

When you are ready to present, produce the cigarette papers and four genuine pencils. After one of these is selected, have someone remove a cigarette paper and decide upon the name of the dead person.

Meanwhile you are busy sorting the correct small pencil in your pocket, let us assume that the red was originally selected, which means that you feel for the pencil which has the point at both ends. This colour, incidentally, is the one most usually selected. Instruct the person to roll the paper into a ball. Whilst he is doing this write the dead person's name on the pocket writer.

Now have him hold the pencil as in 58. This gives you an opportunity to remove the paper from the pocket writer and roll it into a ball, keeping it concealed between your finger and thumb. When he is settled, pick up the blank paper ball and attempt to impale it on the pencil point. This is usually difficult to do the first time and it invariably falls off, but in any event while doing this, switch one pellet for another, so that the paper left on the pencil will be the one bearing the name.

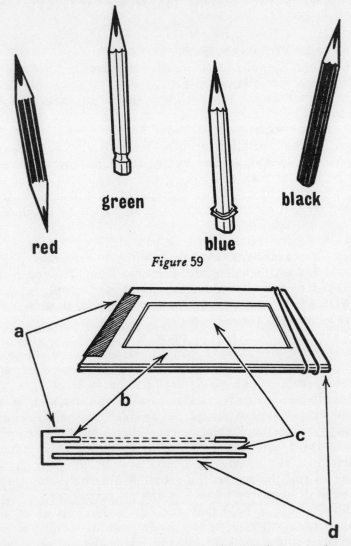

**green**

**black**

**red**

**blue**

*Figure* 59

*Figure* 60 *(a) hinge; (b) top piece with window; (c) cigarette paper; (d) bottom piece of cardboard*

The trick is now finished as far as you are concerned, but added effect can be given by telling the spectator to remove his thumbs from steadying the pencil at this point. As soon as he does this, the pencil will visibly begin to quiver, and the impression gained by everyone will be that the 'spirits' are endeavouring to 'get through'. Someone is now asked to remove the pellet and of course the dead person's name will be seen written on it.

The shaky handwriting will be accounted for by the fact that it is supposed to be spirit writing!

It will at first be quite difficult for you to write on the pocket writer when it is inside your pocket, but confidence is gained after a little practice. In any event, there will be ample time to write the information on the paper, because the person who is to hold the pencil will find it quite a manoeuvre for the first time.

NOTE - See page 48 *'Passe Passe* Cigarette Paper,' for a further description of the cigarette paper switch.


## MAGAZINE TELEPATHY

The performer displays a few assorted magazines or novels on a tray. One of these is freely selected and any word from this magazine is decided upon by a spectator. The performer then picks up a slate and writes on it the *actual* selected word. Sounds impossible doesn't it? Yet seemingly the performer, or 'mentalist' as he may perhaps be called in this case, is able to name one word which has been selected out of many thousands.

Most mental effects have a very simple solution, and it is usually in the presentation that the strength of the performance lies. 'Magazine Telepathy' is no exception.

First of all obtain six different magazines, and duplicates of three of them. Choose them with highly distinctive covers, so that they may be distinguished from a fair distance. Remove the covers from the three duplicates and substitute the cover from three of the genuine ones. Discard the interiors of these genuine magazines. Execute the job quite neatly so they do not appear to have been tampered with. What you now have are six magazines, the covers being all different, but the interiors of three of them are identical with the other three. Pair them off in your mind so that you know which are the duplicates by merely glancing at the covers. The only other requirements are a slate and a piece of chalk.

To PRESENT – Show the magazines and, without actually saying so, indicate that these are all different. Now approach a spectator and have him select any one of the remaining magazines. Stress that his choice is not influenced by you in any way. He can in fact change his mind at this point, if he so desires.

When he has made his final decision, you ask someone else to give you a number, saying that this is to indicate the page in the book.

At this point in order to make things clear, you casually pick up one of the remaining magazines (see that it is the other one of the pair) and tell the spectator roughly how many pages there happen to be. When the page number is known, you indicate what he is to do by casually doing it yourself with the book you are holding. What you do of course is to rapidly turn to the identical page. The spectator imitates your action. Assuming the number was, say, 58, you ask the spectator to count down to the fifth line and look at the eighth word across. You quickly ascertain the word, and still apparently directing the spectator, lay the magazine aside. Remember, your sole object in handling the magazine at all was in order to help the spectator, to show him how to find *his* word.

Ask him to concentrate hard on the word, and ring it round in pencil if necessary. Picking up the slate and chalk, you then endeavour to divine the word he is thinking of – eventually writing it down on the slate.

Have him name the word out loud – you turn round the slate dramatically, revealing your writing on it, and that you have in fact written the actual word he had in mind.

It may be quicker and perhaps easier (depending on the page number thought of) to use only the first word of the line. For instance, if page eight was indicated, count to the eighth line down and use the first word on that line.

Although you have gained the knowledge of the selected word long before the spectator, do not let your audience realize this. You must pretend that you really are endeavouring to read the spectator's mind. Perhaps write a letter or two down on the slate - then erase them - and ask him to concentrate harder; *eventually* you 'get' it and successfully write it down.

## ADDITION MAGIC

A notepad is passed around the audience and someone is asked to write a three figure number in the space shown. Someone else writes a three figure number beneath the first, a third person writes another set of figures and finally a fourth person puts in a similar set of three different numbers.

The pad is now taken to a fifth person who is asked to add up the figures and fill in the total. This he does and writes the total on a slate.

The performer meanwhile does not get the chance to see the writing. He stands on the opposite side of the room, or stage, and picks up another slate.

The person holding the slate is asked to concentrate on the first figure of the total, the performer seems to read his mind and writes it down on his slate. This is done with all the other figures comprising the total. The two slates are turned around simultaneously, and both the totals are seen to read the same.

This mental mystery can be presented as a prediction, or as a mind reading effect as described. If used as a prediction the performer writes the total on the slate before the notebook is passed around, and this is kept covered until the total is arrived at.

But in any event the performer knows what the total will be. How? 'Nothing to it'! The notepad does the trick, though it seems to be quite innocent.

Use a notepad about 4 in. x 3 in. preferably one with a spiral binding (*See 61B*), and on the first page form a sum comprising four sets of three figures. These must be written in different styles to simulate their being written by different people (*See 61C*). Obtain the answer to this sum and write it in pencil on one corner of the slate. Turn the notebook over and open it as if it were the first page once more, place four dots under each other and a bold

line under to indicate where the spectators are to write
their figures (*See 61A*).

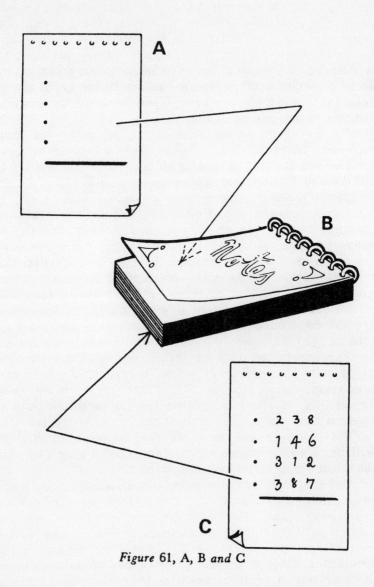

*Figure* 61, A, B *and* C

Equip yourself with pencils and chalk plus a spare slate, and you are ready for the trick.

PRESENTATION - Pick up the notepad and open it at the page which has not been completed; fold back the cover and approach a spectator and ask him to write any three figures against the first dot.

You can then retire to a distance, leaving the notepad, and have this spectator go in turn to three other people who in turn write three figures in the blank space against the dots. The last spectator closes the book and by this time you approach and take it from him.

Go over to another spectator, farthest away, and hand him the book (you have casually turned it over by now) ask him to add the figures and of course the total will come to the number already known by you.

The rest is merely dependent on your ability to act the part of the Mentalist.

Although this turnover ruse is incredibly simple, the spectators will not suspect it. The people who wrote down the figures will genuinely think they are their figures that are being added, and the man who compiles the answer will take your figures for those which were written down by the spectators.

The trick can just as easily be worked in another way, with the performer's assistant, who divines the total from the stage, while the performer does all the work among the spectators. The turn-over is easily camouflaged by the following method; as you take the pad from the third person, you hold it high above your head, ostensibly to prevent your glimpsing its contents by some means. The audience will not detect that it is then placed in the last person's hand the other way up. Do not despise this because of its utter simplicity; it really does score every time.

## YOU WILL SELECT

A visiting card is signed both sides and placed in an envelope with a coloured pencil.

A playing card is now selected, and when the envelope

is opened the name of the selected card has become mysteriously written on the visiting card.

First of all secure a packet of blank visiting cards or business cards, and on top of one of them write, 'the selected card will be the nine of Clubs', (the words 'nine of Clubs' should be written in a different coloured pencil). Place this on the top of a stack of blank cards, and secure with a broad elastic band (*See 62A*).

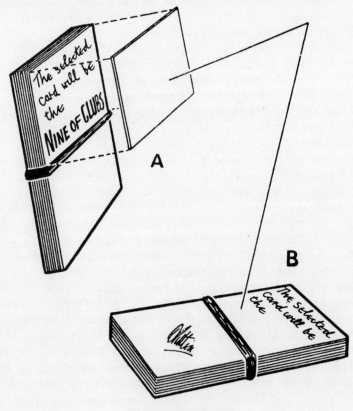

*Figure* 62, A *and* B

Now cut another blank card in half and insert it under the band so that it masks the writing on the card underneath (*See 62B*). The packet of plain cards now appears to be quite innocent.

The card to be forced is on the top of the pack; it need

not necessarily be the nine of Clubs - it can be any one that you previously wrote on the plain card. Have an envelope and the coloured pencil handy, also your own pen for the subsequent writing.

Present the effect like this: Show the packet of visiting cards and write on the top one, as nearly like the duplicate one as possible, 'The selected card will be the...', do not complete the sentence.

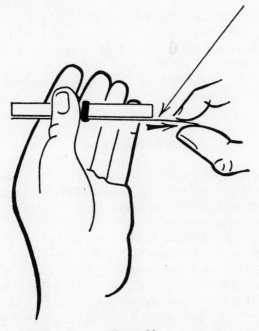

*Figure* 63

Have someone sign their name on the lower part of the card (*See 62B*). The signature actually goes on the bottom part of the card below the band. Turn over the stack of cards and remove the card which you have just signed (*See 63*), and lay it face down on the table. This is also signed across the back by the spectator, and openly placed in an envelope together with the coloured pencil taking great care that you do not let anyone get a sight of the other side at this stage.

It will be necessary to force the card now and the ideal

force to use is that described on page 27, but carry out the procedure as follows.

When the cards are cut, ask the spectator to place the envelope on any pile. If he places it on the one containing the force card, have him place the remainder of the cut pack on top of this.

If he places it on the lower half of the pack, you simply place the upper half, on which the force card faces up, on the envelope, and turn all the cards over. It will be seen that in any event the envelope will be above the force card. After recapitulating what has gone before, the card beneath the envelope is looked at. Then the visiting card inside the envelope is examined and it will be seen that although it has been signed both sides, the name of the card has also become written on it.


## COIN TEST

The Mentalist goes round the audience and borrows several different coins from various people. These are not handled by the performer but are dropped into a large envelope by the lenders.

The envelope is then held above the performer's head, whereupon he immediately tells the dates of the respective coins, the spectators remembering these dates as they are called. When the coins are tipped out of the envelope and handed back to the people who lent them, the dates are checked and the mentalist has correctly divined all the various dates. This is extremely simple. The envelope is double and in the other compartment is a duplicate set of the coins which are to be borrowed. The performer has memorized the dates on each of these. When the coins are tipped out to be verified and returned to their owners, naturally it is the performer's set that are seen; the envelope containing the genuine set is crumpled and placed in the pocket.

# CHAPTER 5 - MISCELLANEOUS MAGIC

The tricks in this chapter are ones that can be performed before a larger audience, making use of props which are visible for a greater distance. You can, however, safely present any of them in a drawing room, although extra care should be taken, especially with regard to angles. That is to say you must watch your spectators' angle of vision, and ensure that no secret prop is visible to them.

There is bound to come a time when you are asked to give a show such as this, and you will find it incumbent on you to offer something more spectacular. You will want to give your audience visual entertainment, and it is with this object in view that the following tricks have been included. They are all extremely good, tried, and tested, 'visible' magic. Indeed if you were to present a conjuring entertainment using the tricks exactly as described and in that order you would find that it would offer a well-balanced, 'meaty' programme, providing excellent opening and closing effects.

## SOFT GLASS

A glass tumbler is shown, and into it is placed a red silk handkerchief. Another silk of a different colour is placed on top of this, and yet a third silk is draped over the top of the glass and secured with a rubber band (*See 64*).

The glass is shown all round, and pretending to melt the bottom of the glass the performer slowly pulls the red handkerchief through the bottom. The tumbler is passed for immediate inspection. The top silk and the one secured by the band are still intact.

You can do this effect quite easily, and the only preparation required is to tie a short length of black thread or fine strong nylon to one corner of the red silk.

Perform this trick as follows – First of all show the glass, tap the bottom and sides to show that it is solid, then stuff the red handkerchief into the glass taking care to ensure that the thread overhangs outside the glass at the back. Place the other silk on top of this, finally capping the glass with the remaining handkerchief, and this being secured with the rubber band. Show it all round, then pretend to bore a hole in the bottom of the glass. Secretly pull on the thread, and this will cause the bottom silk to come out slowly until you can grasp a corner. Continue to withdraw the silk slowly, giving the impression that it is actually penetrating the bottom of the glass.

This manoeuvre will leave the other silks quite intact. Try this pretty effect, without fail – you will even surprise yourself!

**thread**

*Figure* 64

Obtain a metal tube about 2½ in. in diameter by about 5 in. long. This can be made out of a cardboard cylinder, or a beer can, which has had the top and bottom cut away.

The other requirements are two lengths of silken cord (or rope) about six feet long; also three silk hankies. All these props make a colourful effect.

First of all the ropes are shown and the three hankies are tied on to them (*See 65*).

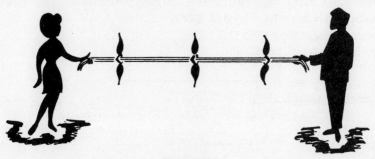

*Figure* 65

The ropes are then threaded through the tube; two spectators assisting by holding the ends of the ropes.

One end is taken from each spectator and tied into a knot over the tube, the ends being handed back.

It will be seen that the silk hankies and the tube are all securely knotted on to the cords.

On the word of command the ropes seem literally to dissolve through the tube *and* the silks, with the silks still in their knotted condition. The cords, tube and silks may be passed for rigorous inspection.

*Figure* 66

This splendid trick is based on a very old principle known as 'The Grandmother's Necklace' - so called because a similar trick was accomplished using very large beads. Its origin is lost in antiquity, but the version now described makes a slick, colourful and up-to-date little illusion.

Only the ropes are prepared. Tie a piece of thread of the same colour once round both ropes, then fold them so that both ends of the same rope are together (*See 66*).

PRESENTATION - Show both ropes and hold them with one hand concealing the thread joint; pull lightly on them to show that they are genuine.

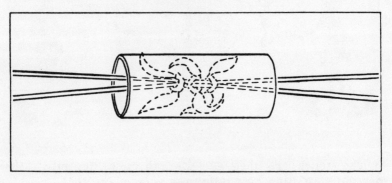

*Figure* 67

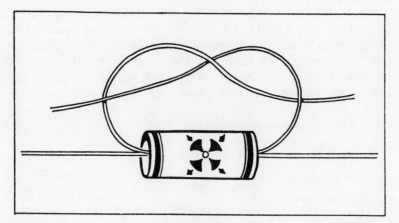

*Figure* 68

*Figure* 69

Now have a spectator tie a silk hanky once around the ropes, and pull this to the centre and over the joint, so that you can now handle them more freely. The other two silks are tied at equal distances along the ropes and the ends given to two spectators who stand each side of you on the stage.

Draw the silks to the centre. Now thread the tube on to the ropes and over the silks (*See 67*). The spectators holding the ropes each give you one end, both of which you take; tie a single knot over the tube, the opposite ends being handed back to the helpers (*See 68*). Say that when you count three, they are to pull sharply on the cords. This they do and the ropes penetrate the tube; the silks fly off but their knots will still be intact (*See 69*).

Of course, the two spectators are left still holding the ends of the ropes which now stretch straight out between them. Naturally everything can be examined at this stage.

# COLOUR CHANGE INK

A small glass half filled with ink is brought forward, covered with a hanky - when the cover is whipped away the ink has changed to water or milk.

Needed for this excellent visual effect is a small glass tumbler and a black plastic or celluloid fake made to fit inside it extending to about half its depth (*See 70B and C*). The fake is made from very thin acetate or film and coloured black.

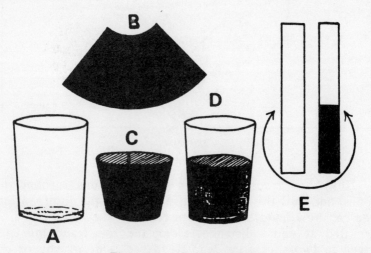

*Figure* 70, A, B, C, D *and* E

Also required is a dip stick made of a thin piece of cardboard - one side of which is perfectly plain white - the other side has about half its length painted black (*See 70E*).

To present the effect you place the plastic fake *inside* the glass and then put water or milk in it to the level of the top of the fake (*See 70D*).

When the glass is picked up and joggled ever so slightly, the liquid inside will appear as ink. Pick up the dipstick being careful only to show its clean side. Dip it in the liquid, but as you do so turn it round and bring it out with the black side showing. Lay the dipstick aside and cover the glass with a handkerchief. As it is whipped away reach into the glass with the finger and take away the fake at the same time. The ink will now be seen to have changed to an entirely different liquid.

## TRICKALOON

This trick is admirably suitable to perform under almost any conditions whether it be close up, in a drawing room or on a stage. It really is a most baffling effect, yet accomplished by the most simple means.

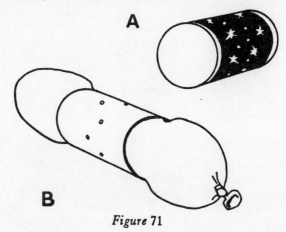

*Figure* 71

The audience is shown a tube about 4 in. high by 3 in. diameter; they see that there are a number of small holes around the centre line of the tube (*See 71A*). Someone is asked to select an airship shape balloon from among several in a dish. It is lowered into the tube and then inflated, so that the tube is held in the middle with the balloon projecting at each end as in 71B. A knitting needle is pushed through one of the holes, completely penetrating the balloon and out at the other side. Yet another needle is pushed through from a different angle. Further needles are also pushed into the tube and thus through the balloon from all sides (*See 72*).

After being shown, the needles are withdrawn one by one, a spectator takes out the last one and himself removes the balloon from the tube. The balloon is seen to be

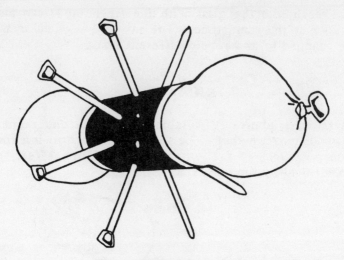

*Figure 72*

**A**

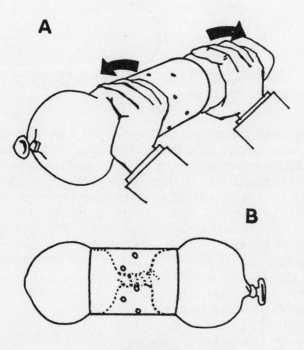

**B**

*Figure 73*

completely undamaged and none the worse for its ordeal.

You will require a supply of large sausage or airship shape balloons as well as several slim steel knitting needles.

The tube can be made of any stiff material, but an ideal way to make it is to cut the neck and base from an empty plastic washing-up-liquid container.  It can be suitably disguised and glamorised by covering it with decorative contact adhesive plastic.  The holes are punched in two rows about 1 in. apart round the centre line of the tube; be sure that the inside of the tube presents a clean smooth surface.

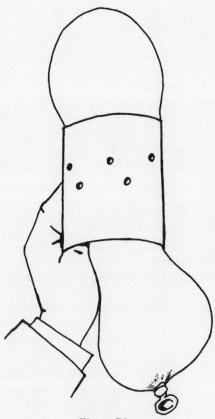

*Figure 74*

Have everything ready on your table and you can now present this little miracle. After the balloon is selected, lower it into the tube and inflate so that it protrudes equally from each end, but do not inflate too hard. Secure the end by tying a knot in it, after which you can freely show the audience the balloon and tube together.

Holding the balloon with one end in each hand as in 73A, secretly twist one end two complete turns away from you. This will cause the balloon to divide into two parts with a waist as seen in 73B. Adjust the tube so that the hole come in line with the waist. The audience should of course be unaware of the secret twist in the balloon. Now hold the balloon upright in the left hand inserting the left thumb in the tube alongside the balloon as shown in 74. Pick up a needle and insert it into a hole from the rear allowing it to be guided by your left thumb around the balloon and out through a hole in the opposite side. At this stage show the balloon all round so that the audience see that the needle really does go right through from side to side. Insert another needle at a different place in the same way but be sure not to foul the balloon, remember that friction will cause the balloon to burst if the needle is rubbed to harshly along its side. Continue with the other needles, carefully inserting them from different angles until it seems an absolute impossibility that the balloon could survive.

To end the trick, withdraw the needles one by one until you come to the last one. At this stage secretly untwist the balloon, then hand it to a spectator to take out the remaining needle himself. The balloon is now taken out of the tube and everything is passed for inspection.

## ROPE RESTORATION

When Robert Orben conducted a poll in the American magic magazine *Genii*, he discovered that the trick most used by conjurors was the 'Chinese Linking Rings' trick. This is, in fact, one of the oldest tricks known to conjurors. But the trick rating second in the poll was the 'Rope Cutting Trick' also a very ancient trick, in fact a simple version of it was described in Scott's *Discoverie of*

*Witchcraft* published in the 17th century. Yet in its present form it is a comparative newcomer to the magic art. Whether or not the trick itself is *more* popular with conjurors than with the audience is left to conjecture, but the fact remains that it is always a popular trick. Consequently the following very good routine is included in this book. The effect is basically simple, being merely that a piece of rope is repeatedly cut and subsequently made whole again.

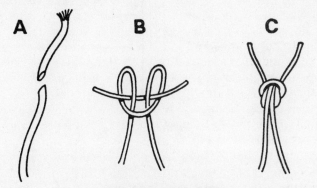

*Figure 75, A, B and C*

A piece of soft white rope about six feet long is required and is prepared as follows. Cut off a piece about 6 in. to 8 in. from the end and form it into a circle, joining the ends with white or colourless rubber cement (the type you use to stick on shoe soles or bind carpets with).

**joins**     **fake knot**

*Figure 76*

A point to remember when using rubber cement is to allow the ends to become tacky before actually joining them. If you have no rubber cement, the ends can be

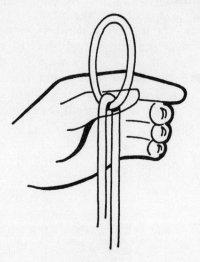

*Figure 77*

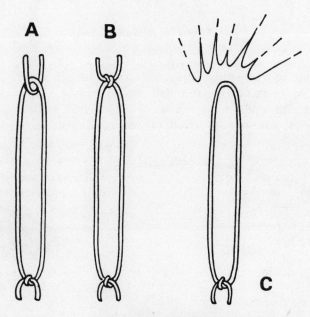

A    B      C

*Figure 78, A, B and C*

neatly sewn with white cotton, or you could use white or transparent adhesive tape.

Another point to note is this: to ensure a strong joint, cut the rope at an angle and join the two broad surfaces (*See 75A*).

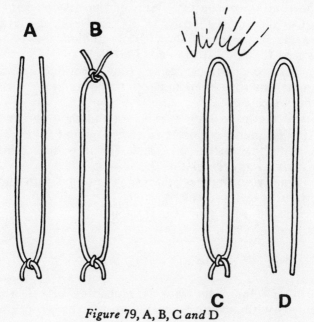

*Figure* 79, A, B, C *and* D

Cut off a further 6 in. piece of rope and tie it on to the centre of the remaining large piece as follows (check 75B and 75C to see that you do get it right). Fold the long piece exactly in half and holding the bight of the rope to the top, fold down the top two inches towards you, forming two loops. Fold these loops away from you together and insert the 6 in. piece through them - pull tightly together and fashion it so that it looks like a genuine knot (*See 75C*).

The next step is to thread the loop of rope you have already made on to the long piece, and the last stage is to join neatly the two ends of this. The finished job should now be as in 76.

Lay this with the loop overhanging the back of the table and armed with a pair of scissors you will be all set to go.

Pick up the rope with the hand masking the intersection of the two loops (*See 77*); the knot should be at the bottom. To the audience it merely appears as a length of rope which has been tied together at the ends.

The routine can best be described in easy stages:

1. Cut the small loop (*See 78A*) and knot this cut piece around the large loop. Show to the audience as being two pieces tied together at the ends (*78B*).

2. Cut the small pieces of rope completely away and show that the rope then appears to be as before, restored into one piece (*78C*).

3. Cut the large loop at the join and show the ends well apart (*79A*), then tie these two ends together (*79B*).

4. Cut the piece of rope forming the fake knot completely away, to restore the rope (*79C*).

5. Finally untie the other (genuine) knot to show the rope is fully restored (*79D*).

6. Pass the rope for examination.


## RING ON THE WAND

The ring on the wand is a transposition effect which, if presented with even a modicum of showmanship, will never fail to register with any audience.

The plot is very simple, being briefly this: the magician borrows a finger ring which is dropped into a small glass, this being covered with a handkerchief and held by a spectator. Now the magician wraps another handkerchief around the centre of a magic wand, and this is given to a second person, who holds the ends very securely. The glass is shaken to prove that the ring is still there, but instantly the magician whips away the handkerchiefs from the glass and the wand, the ring is seen to have vanished from the glass, and is found spinning on the wand.

This is really a 'baffler', and the audience will talk about this feat long after many others are forgotten. First of all prepare a handkerchief as follows: From the centre, sew a strong piece of thread about 6 in. long, on the end of which is attached a cheap ring (*See 80A*). These are usually available from the multiple stores. A gentleman's signet ring is ideal. The other props are quite simple, a small glass tumbler, an ordinary handkerchief (borrow one at the time if you prefer) and a wand - or a pencil would do just as well.

TO PRESENT - The faked handkerchief is placed in readiness in the breast pocket. Begin now by borrowing a ring, this is laid on the palm of the left hand for all to see. Meanwhile remove the handkerchief from the top pocket, and without revealing the duplicate ring hanging from it, drape it over the ring on the hand, so that the borrowed ring and the fake ring lie side by side. Grasp the fake ring through the handkerchief and lift it from the hand, at the same time the left hand closes over the genuine ring. The audience assume that the ring is held safely under the hanky, and to strengthen this belief it is given to someone to hold.

You now place a small tumbler underneath the hanky so that the spectator may drop the ring into it quite safely. Everyone hears it fall, and the glass, still covered, is left with the spectator. The magic wand is now picked up in the right hand, and placed in the left, and as you do this, insert the end into the ring already held there, and bring the left hand still covering the ring into the centre of the wand (*See 80B*).

Drop the ordinary handkerchief over the wand thus covering the ring, then have someone hold the end in a firm grip.

At this point go over what has taken place asking the spectator who is holding the glass to rattle the ring inside it. Make sure that a firm grip is held on both the wand and the glass.

For the final *denouement*, simultaneously whip away both handkerchiefs.

Usually the suspended ring will clink as it leaves the glass, and the effect is quite startling to the onlookers when they see it merrily spinning on the wand in the same instant.

The ring is handed back to its owner and verified that it is in fact the same one, meanwhile you calmly pocket the faked handkerchief.

One little point about the ring - sometimes a wedding or plain type of ring is loaned; in this case see that only the *narrow* part of your duplicate ring is grasped by the spectator.

This splendid effect can be done almost impromptu providing of course you are equipped with the faked ring-in-handkerchief, but nevertheless it still makes a super stage presentation when a wand or musician's baton is used.

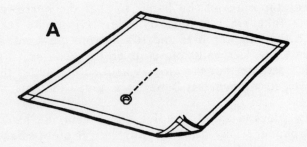

*Figure* 80, A *and* B

# BURNT AND RESTORED PAPER MONEY

Audiences all over the world never fail to delight in seeing conjurors borrow a spectator's hat, handkerchief, or some other personal article, which they proceed to mutilate in some form or another!

Needless to say, the article is always returned unharmed, to the relief of the spectator who loaned it.

The 'Burnt Paper Money' comes in this class of trick, and because it has these humorous potentialities it is well worth the attention of amateur and professional conjurors alike.

As in most other tricks there are many methods by which you can bring about the desired effect. The one about to be described makes use of very simple props, and above all is very simple to do.

To prepare for the effect: Take a ten dollar bill and lightly jot down in pencil the number, just under the flap of an envelope (*See 81A*). Now fold the bill and roll it to a size that will enable you to push it into a cigarette. That brings us to the next step, which is to gently roll a cigarette on the table under slight pressure in order to loosen the tobacco, so that you will now be able to remove most of it with a pair of tweezers. Insert the bill and finish off by replacing some of the tobacco, trying to make the cigarette look as ordinary as possible. It might be necessary to wrap the bill first in a cigarette paper before inserting it in the cigarette; this will prevent it showing through.

Now back to the envelope: fake this by cutting a neat slit at about the centre of the address side (*See 81B*). Place the faked cigarette in the right hand side jacket pocket together with a box of matches.

You are now all set to present the miracle, so begin by borrowing a ten dollar bill, pick up the envelope and make as if to place the bill inside it – but apparently remembering that you omitted to make a note of the number, you appear to read it off while someone jots it down. Naturally you are taking good care to call out the number you have previously written under the envelope flap. If you are able to remember the number you can of course dispense with this subterfuge. Or the number could be written on the thumbnail.

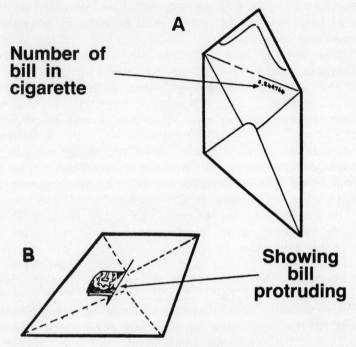

**Number of bill in cigarette**

A

**Showing bill protruding**

B

*Figure* 81, A *and* B

This being done, you proceed to fold the bill in halves then halves again, and then once more, to a size of about $1\frac{1}{2}$ in. x $\frac{1}{2}$ in. In this folded condition the note is inserted into the envelope, but it is also guided through the slit so that the end protrudes outside (*See 81B*).The fingers holding the envelope will also effectively conceal the protruding part of the bill.

In this way the envelope can be shown both sides; now seal down the flap. Hold the envelope against the light and everyone will be able to see that the bill is still there. You can even get someone actually to feel the bill inside the envelope.

Hold the envelope in the left hand and ask someone for the loan of a cigarette which you receive with the right hand. Both hands being fully occupied, you reach into the right hand coat pocket with the right hand and remove the box of matches. This hand is still holding the cigarette, at least that is what the spectators are led to believe. In actual fact as soon as the right hand was out of sight it instantly dropped the genuine cigarette and quickly grasped the fake cigarette and the box of matches, immediately withdrawing them.

This is a perfectly natural action and never suspected by the audience; afterwards they will think that the cigarette never left their sight for an instant. You either give the cigarette to someone to hold or put it between your lips.

Turning your attention to the envelope which has been held all the time in your left hand, you remove a match and set light to one corner. Drop the matches back in the pocket.

As the envelope burns, you slowly slide the bill out and along to one corner, underneath and out of sight, of course. In order to allow the envelope to burn completely you change your grip on to another corner with your other hand, and in doing so carry the money away with your left hand. While everyone's attention is on the burning envelope, you casually allow this hand to dispose of the bill into your pocket. Drop the ashes into a convenient ash tray, and with the last piece of burning envelope light the cigarette.

Quickly stub it out - break it open and reveal the restored ten dollar bill, having the number verified.

You can, of course, have the bill found in an orange in the same way as in the 'Card In Orange' trick to be found on page 14.


## HAT PRODUCTION

The performer borrows a hat, or, if using a top hat, shows it absolutely empty. He then reaches in and produces from it a wide variety of objects such as streamers, silk handkerchiefs, and sweets.

This makes a very good climax to an act, especially

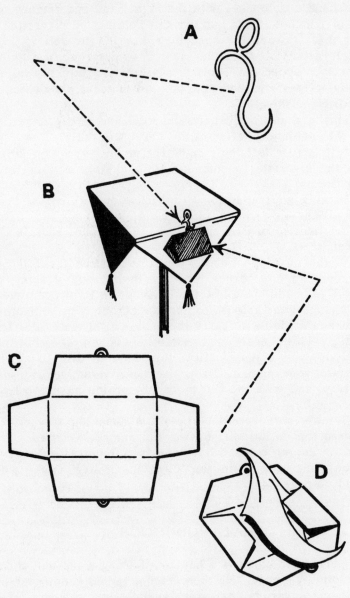

*Figure* 82, A, B, C *and* D

*Figure* 83, A, B, C *and* D

if the production is colourful.

The trick depends on a useful little 'gimmick' which is really the loading device. It is made of thin but strong wire painted black, and bent to form a double hook and loop (*See 82A*). The loop is large enough for the forefinger to engage in it easily.

Now make a fake from black cloth as shown in 82C. Lay this flat on the table and place your load in the centre. Fold the silks neatly and endeavour to condense as much into a small space as possible. Then fold over the left and right sides (*See 82D*). Finally fold over the top and bottom thus securing the load quite safely, press fasteners should be positioned to ensure this. Now attach two loops so the whole load may hang on the loading hook. This hook is placed on the rear edge of the table, loop uppermost, the hook pointing to the rear.

The table itself should be sufficiently draped to mask the load from the front (*See 82B*).

When you are ready to present the effect, show the hat empty and momentarily lay it crown upwards on the table, with the brim of the hat close to the hook.

Show both your hands empty, then turn the hat crown downwards (*See 83A*) but as you grasp the brim of the hat see that your forefinger engages in the loop; the load is thus secretly introduced inside the hat (*See 83B and C*). Practise this deception until you are able to do it confidently and without any fumbling. Once it is safely inside the hat loosen the hook and snap open the fasteners, then proceed to make your production.

Having done this, attempt to cram some of the load back into the hat to prove that quite a bulk came out. Remove it again carrying with it the load container and the hook. The hat can then be passed for inspection if need be.


## RABBIT OUT OF THE HAT

It is usually the ambition of every conjuror to be able to produce a rabbit out of a hat. Indeed it is almost the trade mark of a magician, yet strangely enough this feat is very seldom seen nowadays.

The rabbit to be produced should be fairly small and a special load container must be constructed. It should be made from fairly strong fabric with a stiffened base let into the bottom (*84B shows this container*). The rabbit is placed in this and the top is sealed with a zip fastener. Air holes are provided at the sides, there are also two tags so the container may be suspended from a hook.

Once the rabbit is placed in and settles down in the dark it will be quite docile and remain comfortable. A similar hook to that described in the previous trick ('Hat Production') is provided to suspend the rabbit from the back of the chair (*See 84C*), but the loop can be much wider to allow several fingers·to be inserted.

PRESENTATION – After having made the production of silks and flags out of the hat, they are placed over the back of the chair as if to display them (*See 84D*). At the finish of the hat production, gather these silks into a bundle, at the same time carrying with them the load container, attempting to cram the whole lot back into the hat. The bulk is now too much however, so you reach into the folds of the bundle, release the zip and bring the rabbit into view.

It should hardly be necessary to emphasize that great care should be taken when handling any livestock to ensure that no hurt comes to them. The rabbit, if held by the ears, should be well supported by the other hand taking most of its weight (*See 84A*).

It will be seen that the presentation of 'Hat Production' followed by the production of a live rabbit make a fitting climax to any show. Naturally it is impracticable to have the rabbit suspended on the chair-back throughout the performance. The chair can, however, be brought in by an assistant just as the final production of silks, etc. is made from the hat.

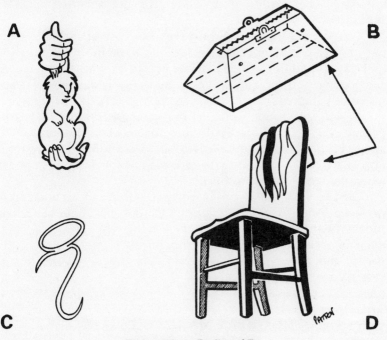

*Figure* 84, A, B, C *and* D

# CHAPTER 6 - ILLUSION MAGIC

In order to make this book as comprehensive as possible and to afford the keen student of magic a thorough grounding in magical knowledge, the following chapter on illusions has been included, but this is the only part of the book which deviates from our policy of describing tricks that are easy to do and which do not require special apparatus.

This aspect of magic however is most absorbing, and the knowledge of one or two illusion principles cannot fail to help the student. Many small tricks are based on these illusion principles and a good many illusions have been likewise adapted from small apparatus effects. Moreover, there will be found one or two amongst those that are described, which can easily be constructed by you. The necessity for adequate rehearsal in presenting this type of magic cannot be too greatly stressed. Especially is this so when assistants are employed.

Timing also plays an important part, and slickness of presentation. The building-up and the practice required successfully to present an illusion are well rewarded, and even in these days when the tendency is to streamline one's props, the audience will always welcome, as a change, a smartly presented illusion.

## THE GREAT MAILBAG ESCAPE

Houdini is generally admitted to have been the greatest exponent of escapology who ever was. Many people have

*Figure 85*

since attempted his marvellous feats. Houdini, however, not only possessed immense technical knowledge of magic, escapology and lock-picking, but he had great physical courage and stamina and it was largely due to these qualities that he was so successful. But nevertheless, the secret behind many of his most astounding feats was incredibly simple, and the 'Great Mailbag Escape' is an instance of this.

The performer is placed in a large (examined) mailbag and the cords at the top are drawn as tightly as possible then tied and sealed.

A screen is placed around, and in a few seconds he makes his appearance, having made his escape from the mailbag, and comes forward with it draped over his arm.

SECRET - The bag is ordinary in every way, but the cord which passes through the eyelets is extra long.

After the bag has been inspected, the performer stands inside the bag and bulls it over him, as he does so he pulls down a loop of cord and places his foot on it (*See 85*). The cord is then pulled tightly, tied and sealed by an assistant. All this time the foot maintains a firm hold of the cord loop, thus enabling him to open the bag and effect his escape. The sack and cord could if necessary again be passed round for inspection.

*Figure* 86

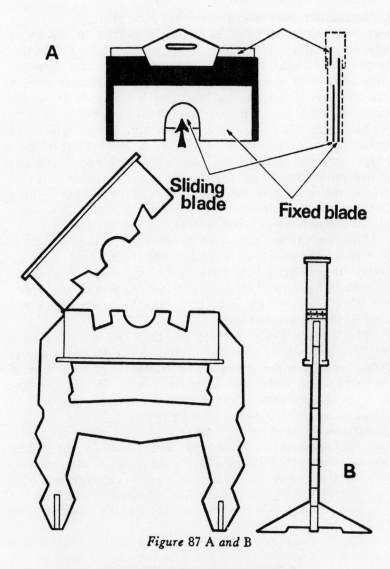

**A**

Sliding blade

Fixed blade

**B**

*Figure* 87 A *and* B

## THE CHINESE GUILLOTINE

A rather impressive-looking Chinese Guillotine (*See 86*) is seen standing on the stage, and to prove that the blade really is sharp the performer places potatoes in the opening and slices them.

A girl is persuaded to place her head through the large centre opening, potatoes again being placed in the small holes at the sides.

The performer slowly pushes the blade down onto the girl's neck, and completely through it. The potatoes at each side are neatly sliced, but the girl is released from the guillotine none the worse for her 'decapitation'!

THE SECRET - This is an ingenious piece of apparatus, and the main secret is in the 'chopper' part which although appearing to be quite genuine, is actually in two parts (*See 87A*). The front piece, or visible blade, is able to move up into the handle. The blade behind being a fixture, it has a circular piece cut out and the upper part of this blade is visible over the top of the handle.

The rest of the apparatus is unprepared and the whole is highly decorated in keeping with traditional Oriental design. It consists of the base (*See 87B*), which is mounted on castors to wheel on and off the stage, and the upper part which is removable to allow the victim to place her head in the centre opening.

The sliding blade is kept in the down position by a headless nail which when removed will allow the blade to slide upwards when coming into contact with the base of the neck; but when the securing pin is in position the chopper can be demonstrated and if a cabbage is placed in the head aperture it will be cut in two.

WORKING - The guillotine is wheeled on to the stage, and the chopper is passed up and down in the frame several times to show the audience that it can be seen through the centre and side openings. A cabbage is placed in the centre with potatoes in the side holes. The blade is dropped rapidly downwards thus slicing the vegetables in half.

The chopper is removed, also the upper part of the frame. The girl places her head in the centre opening and the upper part is replaced. Potatoes are again placed at each side. Meanwhile, the pin is secretly removed so that the visible blade is able to move freely. Always test that the blade slides easily at this point.

Figure 88

After being fitted into the frame it is slowly passed downwards and on to the neck. The moving part will be forced upwards, and the fastened, cut-away, blade passes over and around her neck. The appearance from the front is that the blade has penetrated it.

The chopper is eventually lifted out, gravity causing the sliding blade to fall back into place.

## DOUBLE BOX ILLUSION

A shallow platform which is raised well off the stage is wheeled into view. On it is seen a box, resting on top of this and, folded flat, is another box.

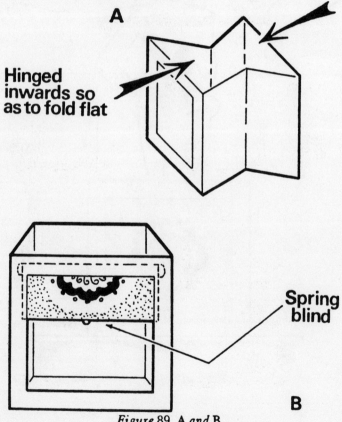

*Figure* 89, A *and* B

The platform is turned in all directions to enable the audience to see all round it.

The boxes are shown to have no bottom or top and are seen to be quite empty, they are then nested one within the other. In spite of this a girl is seen to make a surprise magical appearance from inside the boxes (*See 88*).

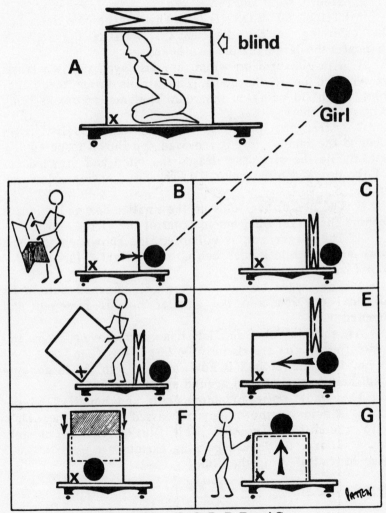

*Figure* 90, A, B, C, D, E, F *and* G

APPARATUS - The base is what it appears to be, just a sturdy but very shallow platform mounted on rubber castors.

The boxes are made to nest one in the other, and constructed so that they can be folded flat quite easily by having the sides hinge inwards (*See 89A*). The larger of the two boxes is faked by having a spring blind in one of its apparently solid sides (*See 89B*).

METHOD OF WORKING - This can best be described by referring to the diagrams as well as the text. X indicates the larger of the two boxes.

1. The platform on which are displayed the two boxes is wheeled on to the stage. The girl is inside the larger box, the blind being to the rear. The smaller box is lying flat across the top (*See 90A*).

2. After the platform has been completely turned around the smaller box is removed and shown to be empty, meanwhile the girl has released the blind and crawled out of the box and hides behind it. The blind has been lowered again (*See 90B*).

3. The performer folds up the smaller box and stands it behind the larger one, but in front of the girl (*See 90C*).

4. The larger box is collapsed and shown empty. The girl is meanwhile hidden behind the upright folded smaller box (*See 90D*).

5. The larger box is now replaced, opened out, in its original position and the smaller box is removed and opened out.

As soon as the smaller box is removed from the platform the girl crawls into the larger box (*See 90E*).

6. The smaller box is now dropped into the larger one and the platform turned around again (*See 90G*).

The whole series of movements and handling of the boxes should be thoroughly rehearsed so that they flow into a continuous routine. This illusion can be cheaply made if large cardboard packing cartons are used. Make a flap instead of using the blind.

# SIMPLICITY ILLUSION

Most illusions are beyond the scope of amateurs and semi-professionals, due to their cost in construction, and transportation difficulties. Here, however, is a simple yet effective illusion which is within the reach of all, costing little or nothing to make up.

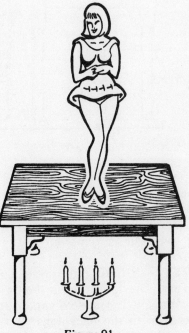

*Figure* 91

The effect is that a girl makes a startling appearance from apparently nowhere.

The audience sees on the stage an ordinary kitchen table; they have a clear view beneath to the curtains at the back, but to enhance the fact that there is nothing concealed beneath, there is a bevy of lighted candles burning merrily away.

The table is set well away from the side wings and

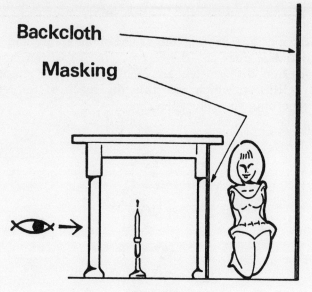

**Backcloth**

**Masking**

*Figure* 92

thus the audience are able to see all around the table, above below and at the sides.

The performer now places a screen on top of the table for an instant; when it is removed a girl is seen standing on the table (*See 91*).

THE SECRET - Almost too simple for words, but the illusion is perfect! The table, while being an ordinary one, is prepared by having a piece of material the same as the backcloth tacked on to the back legs. If the table so faked is placed about 18 in. away from the back curtain, anyone looking directly beneath it will assume there is an unrestricted view. The illusion is heightened by the presence of the candles under the table, apparently placed there to prove that no one can be concealed beneath. But they also *distract* people's attention and add still further to the impression that one does only see the backcloth, and that no mirrors are used. The girl is hidden between the table and back curtain (*See 92*).

The performer has the screen folded at the side of the

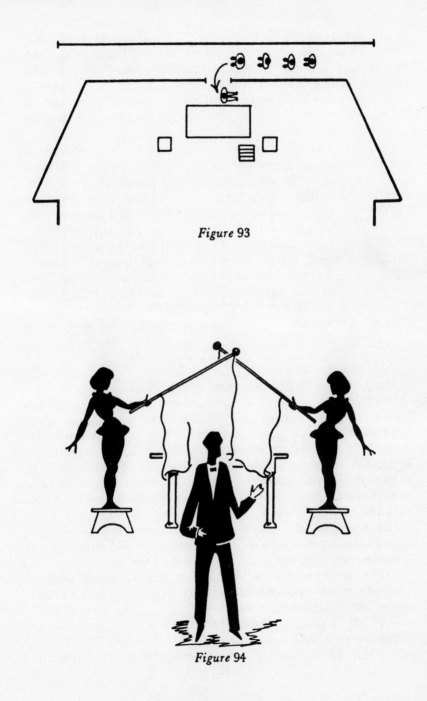

Figure 93

Figure 94

stage, and after tapping his wand on top of the table, the sides and passing it beneath, the screen is placed on top. At this instant the girl climbs on to the table and stands in readiness for the surprise appearance. It is wise to have a small stool behind the table to assist the girl in mounting it; the performer must of course be careful not to pass behind the table.

If more than one person is required to be produced, it can easily be arranged by having a hole cut in the back cloth so that each subsequent person takes up a position behind the table, coming from backstage whilst the one before them is being 'produced' (*93 shows a plan of this layout.*)

Instead of a screen it is possible to have two girls suitably dressed, standing on a stool each side of the table. They each have a banner which is held up so that they overlap until the appearing person is ready in position. This makes an ideal setting for a production of the whole cast of a stage show either at the beginning or as a finale (*See 94*).

## AERIAL BROOM SUSPENSION

The illusionist shows two broomsticks and holds them upright on a base set on the stage. The lady assistant now steps onto a small stool placed between them, resting her arms on the brooms (*See 95A*). She is hypnotized by the magician and the stool is taken away, but the girl remains effortlessly suspended and supported by the two brooms, as in 95B.

Now one of the brooms is taken away and to everyone's surprise she apparently defies the law of gravity and stays suspended in mid air (*See 96*).

The performer now lifts her to a position so that she reclines at an angle of 45 degrees still suspended by some invisible influence (*See 97*).

Finally she is placed into a horizontal position and amazing as it may seem the girl stays suspended in thin air (*See 98*). To conclude, the girl is lowered to the upright position, the other broom and stool are replaced, she is 'dehypnotized' and steps down off the stand.

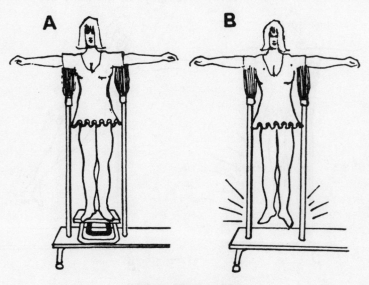

*Figure* 95, A *and* B

METHOD - The secret lies in two factors which are unknown to the audience, the girl wears a special harness beneath her dress enabling her to remain rigid on the broom. Attached to the harness is a special ratchet device which enables her body to be placed at an angle and on the horizontal. One of the brooms is faked, really it is a broom made out of a metal rod suitably camouflaged. One end is inserted into a special socket let into the base. The other end of the broom has a hole drilled to take the plug which is located on the arm pit section of the harness.

PRESENTATION - The base is wheeled on, the brooms shown, then the girl steps onto the stool, the brooms are placed under each armpit. Actually one end of the broom sockets into the hole in the base. While adjusting the broomhead under the armpit, the plug is located in the socket on the end of the rod. This will now support the girl. Remove the stool - girl remains suspended. Remove the genuine broom, toss it onto the stage, girl still stays supported. Reach under girl and locate ratchet lever, pull down to disengage, raise girl to 45 degrees angle allowing tongue on the end of lever to engage in the next groove.

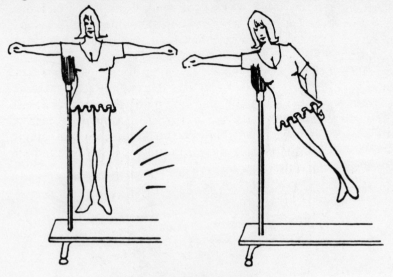

*Figure* 96 *and* 97

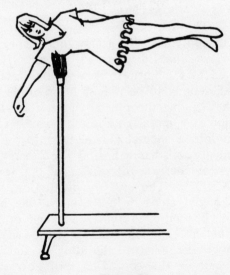

*Figure* 98

Finally lift girl horizontal, again using ratchet lever disengaging first then allowing it to fall into the next cut away part. To lower the girl pull on lever keeping it well under tension, lower her. As stool is placed beneath, she draws herself upright, whilst you knock out the pin from broomhead. She will be able to step down from the stand, but it is inadvisable to make her walk more than a couple of steps due to the restriction of the harness.

APPARATUS - The base is simply a low platform made to take the weight of the girl. Usually it is on castors so that it can be easily pushed onto the stage. Some performers dispense with the platform, but in this case a special socket unit will have to be sunk into the stage proper - this is normally only practical on well-equipped stages or long runs.

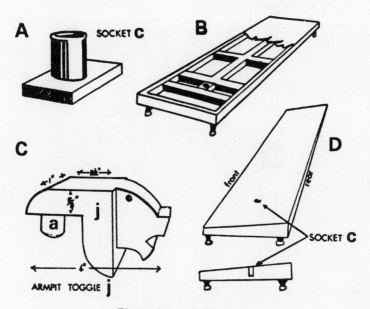

*Figure* 99, A, B, C *and* D

The base should be thick enough to allow the broom handle to sink in at least 2½ in. In order to cut down weight the base can be merely a light wood frame covered with ply, but cross membered to give strength (*See 99B*). The socket should be let in. It has been found that a mast socket available from boat builders, used on launches etc. is quite suitable (*See 99A*).

The *fake broom* is made of 1¼ in. high-tensile steel rod 5 ft. 9 in. long (*See 100*). The socket in the base is just big enough for a close fit round the broom. One end of the broom is drilled a little over ½ in. x 1 in. This is to receive the armpit pintle shown as *(a)* in *101*. The bass or bristles are built round the drilled end which rests just below the surfaces (*See 100*).

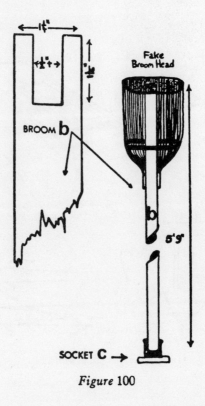

*Figure 100*

136

The *harness* is attached to the jointed body arm and is made of steel (*See 101*) consisting of a waistband *(d)* and steel crutch band *(e)*. The waistband passes around the girl's waist being secured by an adjustable strap *(f)*. A shoulder strap *(g)* is attached to the waistband passing from the rear and over the left shoulder down to the front.

The steel crutch *(e)* acts as rear support passing between the legs ending in an upward curve and is held secure against the abdomen by the strap *(h)*.

A final strap *(i)* encircles the thigh and is attached to the lower part of the jointed body arm *(n)*.

The *jointed body arm* consists of three main parts; the armpit toggle *(j)* the upper arm and ratchet lever *(m)* and the lower hip joint and arm *(n)*.

The armpit toggle is shown in greater detail in 99C and is made from steel tooled to shape, 4 in. overall, length of upper plane surface 2½ in. x 1 in. width. This is hinged to the upper arm by a pin passing through both.

The *upper arm (k)* is shown in 102A and as a plan view in 103A. It is hinged to the armpit toggle as described, and extends down to the hip joint *(l)*. The knuckle moves round an angle of 90 degrees from the vertical to the horizontal.

The *upper arm ratchet (m)* forms part of the upper arm and is attached to its underside, terminating in a finger lever. When pulled downwards the spring is put under tension and this clears the ratchet free from the armpit toggle. As already described, by moving the girl into the angled and horizontal positions the ratchet tongue will engage in the two positions on the toggle (*See 103B*).

*The lower hip joint and arm (n)* is merely an extension of the upper arm and hinges back and forwards only to enable the girl to move her leg. The knee strap is attached to the end of this (*See l and i*).

NOTE - The apparatus should be made sturdy enough to support the weight of the girl and depends on the measurements of the assistant to be used - the straps allowing for extra adjustment.

As a guide, the jointed body arm should extend from the armpit to just above the knee. 102B shows the harness in position on the girl. There is also a strap which supports

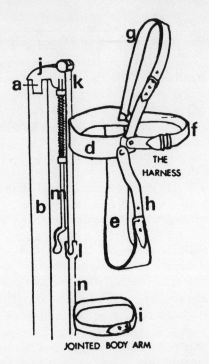

THE HARNESS

JOINTED BODY ARM

*Figure* 101 (*a*) *pintle;* (*b*) *fake broom;* (*d*) *waistband;* (*e*) *crutch band;* (*f*) *waist strap;* (*g*) *shoulder strap;* (*h*) *abdomen strap;* (*i*) *thigh strap;* (*j*) *armpit toggle;* (*k*) *upper arm;* (*l*) *hip joint;* (*m*) *ratchet and lever;* (*n*) *lower hip joint and arm*

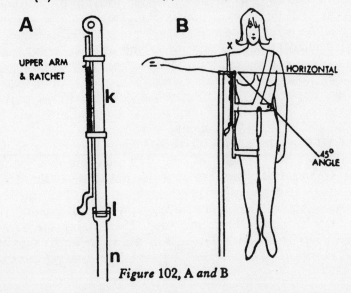

**A**

UPPER ARM
& RATCHET

**B**

HORIZONTAL

45°
ANGLE

*Figure* 102, A and B

138

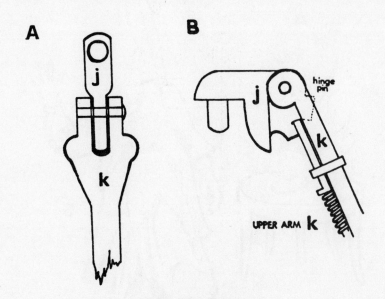

*Figure* 103, A *and* B

the girl's arm on top of the armpit toggle, marked X in 102B.

The straps, metal waistband and crutch are all heavily padded with foam rubber as is the upper surface of the armpit toggle. A hole should be cut in the girl's dress so that the ratchet lever can easily protrude.

When the girl is raised to the horizontal position she will have to keep her legs extended by muscular power. It is more easily achieved by crossing the ankles. Nevertheless, this position is very tiring and it is inadvisable to maintain it for long.


## LIVING HEAD ILLUSION

An awe-inspiring spectacle, the 'Living Head Illusion' has a touch of the macabre about it, which makes it particularly effective.

The Sorcerer cuts the head from his assistant and transports it across the stage and places it in full view on a table, whereupon it begins to talk and answer questions.

*Figure* 104, *A and B*

This is quite a gruesome sight, because the table itself is seemingly an innocent affair. There is an unrestricted view between the legs, and the whole effect of a bodyless head is undeniably realistic.

It is a very old illusion and was a great favourite among the conjurors of the eighteenth century. The main secret lies in the special table, and this is so constructed as to make use of a very clever mirror-reflection principle. A careful study of the drawings will reveal the method by which the illusion is effected. 104A shows how the table and head look to the audience. 104B gives an impression of the headless man.

105 shows a plan view of the table; (x) and (y) are two mirrors set at an angle, this creating an impression that the table affords an unrestricted view beneath, (z) is a hole cut in the table top through which a hidden assistant thrusts his

head. The mirrors, of course, effectively conceal the body. A close study of the sketch (*See 105B*) will explain how this principle operates.

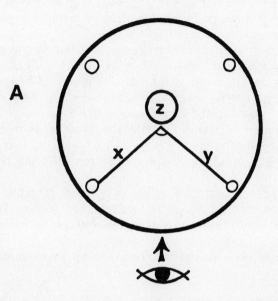

**A**

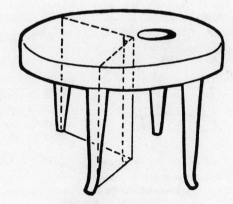

**B**

*Figure* 105, A *and* B

The leaded edges of the mirrors are concealed by the two front legs and the point where they meet is masked by the central leg.

A second assistant is used to effect the decapitation part. He has a special expanding coat and on his shoulders is built a framework to enable him to withdraw his head into the dummy shoulders (*See 106B*).

The tureen shaped cover shown in *106A* is big enough to go over the head, and as soon as this is done, he ducks down into the framework. The sword is passed beneath the cover to apparently sever the head, which is now carried to the table and located exactly over the hole.

The hidden assistant beneath the table now thrusts up his head and the cover is removed to reveal it, whereupon the performer indulges in a conversation with the bodyless head.

The head is removed eventually, and returned to its rightful owner who seems none the worse for his experience! The reverse moves take place to accomplish this.

Naturally both assistants are made up to resemble each other.

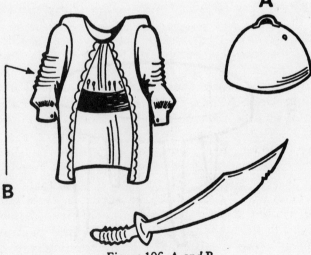

*Figure* 106, A *and* B

# CHAPTER 7 - SHOWMANSHIP AND PRESENTATION

This is probably one of the most important chapters in the book. Most people with a modicum of common sense and knowing how a trick is done will be able to do that trick, but unless they have bothered to study its *presentation*, the difference will show like the difference between an accomplished violinist and a person who is just taking lessons on the fiddle! They may both be using the same instrument but the tune certainly sounds different.

It is necessary to 'sell' your act the whole time that you are performing, in your appearance, your actions, and in your speech. You should 'register' from the word go. This means that your opening trick should be strong, it should fit your own personality and it should be a trick which you are confident in performing. If it goes well the audience will applaud, and this serves to break down that invisible barrier which exists between the audience and the performer when he makes his entrance. If this barrier is broken down, the path of the performer is made easier in his next effect, because by then the audience are 'with' him. It follows, then, that the quicker this is done the better it will be. That is why many performers favour quick tricks as opening effects, and if surprise forms part of the emotions registered by the audience, their attention will be secured at once. Having gained their attention, it is up to you to give your best to maintain their interest, and if your offering is pleasing and entertaining you cannot fail to win applause.

Having made your entry it is a good plan to build up with each successive trick until the climax is reached, so that your closing effect is a real winner.

The *last* trick is what your audience will probably remember you by, for it will be their last impression of you. Endeavour to make it an applause-getter, so strong that the audience are left in no doubt that you have finished.


## MISDIRECTION

Misdirection can be best described by an example; suppose a magician wishes to make a handkerchief disappear, and at the crucial moment arranges for a terrific bang at the back of the theatre. Everyone's attention is riveted on his hands and his handkerchief at one instant, and in the next everyone's attention is drawn to the back of the hall. It is an easy matter, then, for the conjuror to dispose of his 'hanky' without anyone being any the wiser as to where it went.

Of course, this example of misdirection is a little far-fetched, but it will serve to draw your attention to the fact that it is possible to make the audience do something which they did not expect to do a moment earlier. Now supposing a conjuror holds a pistol in his hand and fires it at the handkerchief he wishes to 'vanish,' it then becomes more logical; the audience will readily accept the disappearance, despite the noise from the gun, which all the same served to misdirect their attention for that one moment.

But misdirection is not confined to guns and bangs and there are many ways in which it can be used. For instance, your patter or dialogue can serve to distract people's attention; whilst they are busy listening to your chatter, little dodges will go unperceived. To carry this one stage further, if you can contrive to make the audience laugh at any given point, this is also ideal misdirection; in being amused for that instant they give you time to cover that awkward move.

There are countless other ways in which you can achieve a desired result by doing something totally different. Suppose you wish to secure a secret load which is hanging behind your table. Pick up the table and carry it nearer to your audience. This is a perfectly natural move, but under the cover of the action you have the opportunity to steal the load. Be as natural as possible in your performance. Do contrive to find an excuse for your hand to go to your pocket if you need to secure something. Or, if you wish to dispose of say a small object on to your table, pick up your magic wand; at the same time leave the object there. Although the real reason for going to your table was to 'ditch' the object, the audience are led to believe that you required to pick your wand up. Having done so, however, be sure that you make use of it. Tap a piece of apparatus with the wand, wave the wand over it, and so on.

A common fault among conjurors, when they practise a sleight is to blink just when the important move takes place. You see they even try to misdirect themselves! But, after all, misdirection is not really so difficult is it? Before you put a trick over on an audience consider what has been said, then study your presentation and see if those awkward moves are as covered as they should be.

Sooner or later, misdirection will become second nature to you, and ultimately you will find yourself developing certain mannerisms and a special style in performing which will make itself apparent.

This is when you will find that your performance has become individual - it will be just you. So be sure that you study these problems from the start. Aim at excellence, for the final result will make you an 'Expert Conjuror', a 'Polished Performer'.


## PATTER

The main purpose of patter, as far as the audience is concerned, is to assist them in following the routine of your tricks. But is has already mentioned that patter in itself can serve to cover the awkward moves in your tricks and act as a form of misdirection.

This book has avoided written patter because it is felt that one's dialogue is a personal thing. One person's phrasing can always sound awkward if another person uses it. Patter, above all, should flow perfectly naturally and not sound dull and parrot-like, as if it were obviously learnt by heart. This does not mean that patter should *never* be learnt by heart, for the most successful after-dinner speakers, comedians, and conjurors know their script, or speech, off pat. It must always *sound* spontaneous, impromptu, or if you like extempore, however; that is the secret of good patter. It must be used sparingly, seem to sparkle, be amusing or interesting, and it should never be in bad taste.

If a trick should go wrong, and it could happen to the best of performers, do not get flustered, or look depressed, but have a witty comment ready to make. Invent special phrases to use on such an occasion, so that you will not be at a loss, for you can sometimes turn your misfortune to good advantage, and at least it will get you out of trouble. For instance if you inadvertently drop something - you could say as you pick it up - 'this trick takes a lot of picking up...' Make your patter in itself useful, make it apply to the trick in question; in this way you will maintain interest throughout your performance, but ensure that what you have to say is worth saying, watch the quality of your voice and the character of your delivery and remember that in speaking as in all things, practice makes perfect.

If you address your remarks to a point about two-thirds of the way back in your audience, you will find that your voice will carry and be heard by everyone. Be sure also to see that you bring everyone into the picture by looking at various parts of the audience, otherwise you will fall into the trap of playing only to one person.

This subject is so vast that it would take too much time to do more than touch the fringe of it. A good plan is to try to get the opportunity of hearing yourself speak. The way to do this, if you have not got a tape-recorder is to beg, borrow or steal one. Please do not take this too literally!

Whilst it is not recommended that other performers' material should be copied, ideas can be obtained by watching television and listening to the radio. After all, most jokes and comedy situations are variations on a basic theme.

It is now generally known that most topline comedians have their scripts written for them by professional script writers. There are also script writing services available for other acts, including magicians, and these can be found in the advertising section of *The Stage*.

Finally your local Dramatic Society can be a wonderful source of practical knowledge of the theatre. Therefore, we do advise the student to consider joining such an organization. It will provide training in elocution and the basic abilities required in all who aspire to be that 'Expert Conjuror and Polished Performer'.

## FINAL HINTS AND TIPS

A good plan when arranging a show is to have a small card on which is written the name of each trick in the order they are going to be presented. Place this on the table and it will serve as a reminder, ensuring that the tricks are being worked in their proper sequence. Keep this card for later reference and if the date and place of the performance are also written on it, you will be able to check up on your last show if you have to perform at the same place again.

In fact, if you are really methodically minded, it is a wonderful idea to keep a card index of all your performances. Set it out systematically with the name; place; date; time; duration of show; number of appearances; how to get there; who to contact; performance conditions (i.e. stage, dressing room, piano, microphones, curtain arrangements etc.); fee; tricks performed; type of audience; other artistes and so on.

When setting out the props on the table, always lay out the last trick first. This will ensure that the various pieces of apparatus are readily to hand when needed, thus obviating fumbling and awkwardness during the show.

In the absence of an assistant, endeavour to have an extra table on which to dispose of the discarded props. A chair would suffice if no table is available.

A makeshift table can be made from two chairs placed

a short distance apart, back to back. Balance a tray across the top. You will then be able to set out the props on one chair-seat, using the tray as the table proper, and placing the objects, as they are finished with, on the other seat.

But having your own table looks nicer and lends the professional touch. Perhaps it is better still to use a modern sort of dinner trolley, preferably one which can collapse to a smaller size for ease in transportation. After your apparatus is set it can be wheeled on and off with all your props intact and in one place. This is particularly suitable when working in cabaret conditions.

Obviously it is common courtesy not to leave the stage or room untidy after your performance is finished especially where other artists are to follow you, or when performing in a private house.

'Leave the audience wanting more' is a good maxim but in any case it is bad manners to overplay your time when working with other artistes. Nevertheless it is wise to keep a spare trick available in case of emergency.

May you have many hours of enjoyment from this fascinating hobby - there are always new things to see and new tricks to work and you will also find there is a wealth of good fellowship among conjurors.

Good Showing!

HARRY BARON.

---

# GLOSSARY

There are many words used throughout this book which, although they are known very well to conjurors, are not generally in common usage. In order to assist the student in magic, a short glossary has been compiled. Naturally there are many more such words and phrases peculiar to magic but this list is confined to those which have actually been used in these pages.

APPEARANCE - The result of a production - 'The girl made a sudden appearance from an empty box.'

ACT - A complete programme or presentation (an act), not used in the sense of 'to act'.

APPARATUS - Props (properties). Items used by the performer - magical equipment.

ACQUITMENT - A series of moves, or a manoeuvre, during the presentation of an effect, mostly applicable to sleight of hand, more usually to vanish an article.

BACKS - The pattern sides of playing cards. Conversely the FACES are the fronts: the sides which depict the value.

BILLET - A small piece of paper on which is written information. Mostly used in mental effects.

BIGHT - Appertaining to rope or ribbon, etc. If a piece of rope is doubled in half, the centre is known as the bight.

BOTTOM CARD - Referring to the bottom card of a pack: the opposite to TOP CARD, designating the topmost card of the pack.

CONJUROR'S CHOICE - (*See page 14.*) A spectator's choice which, although ostensibly a free one, is in fact determined by the conjuror.

CUTTING - 'To Cut the Pack,' is to divide the cards. 'To Complete the Cut,' is to remove a quantity of cards from the top of the pack and place them on the bottom.

DITCH - To dispose of, usually secretly; to leave behind.

EFFECT - The general impression the trick makes on the audience. Its appearance, what it looks like to the spectator.

FACES - See BACKS.

FAKE OR FEKE - See also GIMMICK. The part of the apparatus which is prepared in such a way as to make possible the result of the trick. TO BE FAKED denotes that the apparatus or prop is seemingly ordinary but has been altered to create the desired effect.

FALSE SHUFFLE - The cards are mixed (shuffled) in a seemingly innocent way, but in actual fact the pack order remains undisturbed.

FEATURE - A trick given a special point in the programme, it is highlighted - 'to feature an effect'.

FIRST FINGER - (FOREFINGER) (INDEX FINGER). Denotes finger next to the thumb. The others are designated 2nd, 3rd and 4th - the fourth being the little finger.

FOREFINGER - See above.

FREE - Signifies that the spectator has been given a wholly free choice; his selection, not having been influenced by the conjuror.

GIMMICK - Describes an apparatus used by the conjuror but which is unknown to the audience. Also denotes FAKING - 'the rope was gimmicked'.

GRANDMOTHER'S BEADS - Very old principle in magic (*See page 100*). Describes trick NECKLACE where large beads were threaded on string and subsequently removed while the ends were held. Makes use of two strings doubled back, and forms basis of many tricks today.

INDEX FINGER - See FIRST FINGER.

INDIFFERENT- Denotes card other than those designated in the experiment CARD at the time, i.e. the Four Aces are specific cards - all others are indifferent.

KEY CARD - A card predetermined, which will assist in the location of another; could also be specially faked (see LOCATOR or SHORT CARD).

LOAD - A collection of material usually compressible such as SILKS, SPRING FLOWERS, RIBBONS assembled neatly together for subsequent PRODUCTION. Also TO LOAD, which means to introduce the LOAD into, say, a special compartment, usually done secretly. LOADING DEVICE is gimmick enabling conjurors to do this.

LOCATOR - As in KEY CARD, but TO LOCATE means to find a card or establish and control its position in the pack.

MENTALIST - Name given to performer who presents effects of a mental nature (MIND READER).

MISDIRECTION - See page 144.

MOVES - Manoeuvres executed by the conjuror to bring about a trick.

ONE AHEAD - A principle in magic, used mainly by mentalists. (*See page 80.*) The performer is 'one ahead' of the audience, securing knowledge from a note he is reading, while supposedly calling off the previous one.

OPERATOR - Name given to PERFORMER; usually applicable to SLEIGHT OF HAND.

OVERHAND - The shuffle most commonly used; see page 22 for description.

PACK - The complete set of 52 cards. (Also DECK.)

PACK ORDER - Signifies arrangement of pack.

PALM - To conceal some small object in the hand secretly.

PERFORMER - The Conjuror - Mentalist - Operator - Magician - Artiste.

PELLET - Sometimes called a BILLET, but more properly this is the size of a pea - could be a 'pellet of wax', a rolled-up cigarette paper, etc.

PRODUCTION - 'To make a Production' is to cause an appearance of something, a girl, livestock, or goods such as silks, etc. Production is the name given to object after it is produced.

PRINCIPLE - Basic method by which a trick is accomplished.

PREPARE - The faking of an object, or to arrange and set articles, ready for the performance. 'The pack is prepared as follows:'

PRESENTATION - See page 145*. TO PRESENT means to show the trick.

PROPS - See Apparatus. (PROPERTIES).

RIFFLE - Applies to cards. They are held in the left hand as if for dealing and the 2nd finger of the right hand bends the top edge upwards allowing them to fall consecutively. A RIFFLE SHUFFLE is where the cards are divided into two piles, held one part in each hand and each half is 'riffled' into the other, finally being squared up - thus the cards have been mixed or shuffled.

SLEIGHTS- ACQUITMENTS performed by the conjuror in order to accomplish a desired effect. SLEIGHT OF HAND as applied to sleights or moves usually secret, using the hands.

SHOWMANSHIP - See page 143.

SHORT CARD - Card which has been cut short (*see page 6*), this then acts as a Key Card or Locator. Also similar are WIDE CARDS, NARROW CARDS, LONG CARDS, each performing the same function.

SHUFFLE - To mix the cards.

SILK - A silk handkerchief (HANKY) in many colours and sizes.

SQUARE UP- After the cards have been dealt, counted or shuffled they are then formed into a neat stack again.

STEAL - To secure any object secretly unknown to the audience.

SWITCH - To exchange one object secretly for another of a similar kind, i.e. a faked pack can be switched for a genuine one.

TABLE TRICK - An effect suitable mainly for an audience grouped or sitting around a table. A close up effect.

THICK CARD - Made by sticking two cards together and used as a locator or key card (refer also to SHORT CARD). A makeshift THICK CARD can be temporarily made by moistening the back of any card and allowing the JOKER to adhere to it.

TOURNIQUET - Name given to a very old acquitment or sleight causing the vanish of small articles: see page 55.

TOP CARD - See BOTTOM CARD.

TRANSPOSITION - A basic effect in magic; one article is made to change magically with another.

VANISH - Another basic effect; to cause any object to disappear: 'the silk was vanished'.

(The keen student will realize that magic is generally comprised of these BASIC EFFECTS and nearly all presentations are variations of PRODUCTIONS, EVANISHMENTS, TRANSPOSITIONS, PENETRATIONS, and LEVITATIONS.)

---

# MAGICAL SOCIETIES

Assistance in the procurement of materials as well as help and advice for the young magician can be obtained in the USA through the International Brotherhood of Magicians, 103 N. Main Street, Bluffton, OH 45817-0089, and in the United Kingdom - The Hon Secretary, H. J. Atkins, Kings Garn, Fritham Court, Fritham, Lyndhurst, Herts SO43 7HH.

Chapters of this exceedingly helpful organization, known as *Rings*, are located in many cities around the world.

In the United Kingdom the Magic Circle at the following address should be contacted -

The Magic Circle, c/o The Victory Services Club, 63/79 Seymour Street, London W2 2HF, England

# MAGICAL MAGAZINES

There are a number of magical magazines published in the USA and the United Kingdom and the articles and advertisements published will provide up-to-date information. Here are a few of the magazines to which you can subscribe -

Abracadabra ( weekly), Goodliffe Publications, 150 New Road, Bromsgrove Worcester B60 2LG.

Genii (monthly) P.O. Box 36068, Los Angeles, CA 90036, USA.

The Linking Ring - this magazine is specifically for members of the International Brotherhood of Magicians. See the address given on page 155

The Magic Manuscript. A bi-monthly magazine published by Louis Tannen Inc, 6 W. 32nd St., 4th Floor, New York, N.Y. 10001, USA

The Magic Circular - specifically for members and associate members of the Magic Circle, London. See address on page 155.

Opus Magazine. A chatty journal which is published monthly. Write to Opus, 11 Pedlars Walk, London N7 9PT.

# MAGICAL DEALERS

There are many firms which deal specifically in items for the conjuror. Here are just a few selected at random. If writing for information it is wise to include sufficient stamps to cover a reply.

The majority of magic dealers publish catalogues and newsletters and these will help to keep you informed on the latest developments in magic. It is very easy to read the glowing and exciting advertisements published by magic dealers and it is equally easy to send off for the latest 'miracle'. Good magicians and particularly good close up magicians rarely rely on unusual props and apparatus. There is little to be gained from watching a performer who uses nothing but garishly painted and blatantly feked magical apparatus. Although the publisher of this book is a magic dealer himself his advice is to read magic books, watch skilled performers, attend lectures given by experienced professionals and watch magical video cassettes that are designed to teach the elements of magic and sleight of hand. Here are a few magic dealers selected at random -

Louis Tannen Inc, 6 W.32nd St., New York, NY 10001, USA.

The Supreme Magic Company, 64 High Street, Bideford, Devon EX39 2AN, England.

Kaymar Magic, 106A High Street, Billericay, Essex CM12 9BY, England.

Davenports, 7 Charing Cross Underground, The Strand, London WC2N 4HZ, England.

Alan Alan's Magic Spot, 88 Southampton Row, London WC1, England.

The International Magic Studio, 89 Clerkenwell Road, London EC1, England.

Magic Books by Post (Specialist in magic books but mail order only. No callers). Phone or write information, 29 Hill Avenue, Bedminster, Bristol BS3 4SN, England. Telephone (0272) 774409.

# MAGIC CONVENTIONS

Almost every weekend of the year there is a Magic Convention being held somewhere. If you attend a convention you will be able to view the latest magical effects for sale, attend lectures on close up and stage magic and meet and mingle with experienced and inexperienced performers. Details of Magic Conventions and their venues are published in magic magazines.

# BIBLIOGRAPHY

Books which describe magic tricks and how to do them, believe it or not, run into many thousands and most of them are directed to the experienced conjuror, or advanced amateur. Surprisingly enough only a small portion of this wealth of magic literature is written for the learner of magic.

The titles which follow here, although not necessarily for the beginner, have been specially selected to assist the reader to further most easily his magical knowledge, for most of them are generally available to the public.

CARD TRICKS WITHOUT SKILL, Paul Clive (*Faber*), Cards

THIRTEEN STEPS TO MENTALISM, Tony Corinda (*Supremem Magic*), Mentalism

MAGIC AS A HOBBY, Bruce Elliott, (*Faber*), General Magic

CLASSIC SECRETS OF MAGIC, Bruce Elliott (*Faber*), General Magic

MATHEMATICS, MAGIC AND MYSTERY, Martin Gardner (*Dover*),

ENCYCLOPEDIA OF CARD TRICKS, Jean Hugard (*Faber*), Cards

ROYAL ROAD TO CARD MAGIC, Jean Hugard (*Faber*), Cards

MODERN MAGIC MANUAL, Jean Hugard (*Faber*), General Magic

CARD CONJURING, Wilfred Johnson (*Dover*), General Magic

CONJURING, Wilfred Johnson (*Foyles*), General Magic

SHOWMANSHIP AND PRESENTATION, Edward Maurice (*Goodliffe*), Stage Technique

COMEDY, PATTER AND DIALOGUE (Numerous), Robert Orben (*Orben*), Patter

SCARNE'S MAGIC TRICKS, John Scarne (*Constable*), Cards

COME A LITTLE CLOSER, Peter Warlock (*Kaymar*), Close-up Tricks

A BOOK OF MAKE-UP, Eric Ward (*French*), Theatrical Make-up

THE TARBELL COURSE OF MAGIC, Harlan Tarbell (Louis Tannen Inc), seven volumes comprehensively covering the entire field of conjuring

(For a comprehensive list of all major magic books available contact Magic Books by Post and request their catalogue of titles. Their address appears on page 158).

Some of the books listed above may be difficult to obtain. Should you join a magic club you will probably be able to find them in the club library.